30 DAYS TO ONLINE PR & MARKETING SUCCESS

The 30 Day Results Guide to Making the
Most of Twitter, Facebook, LinkedIn,
and Blogging to Grab Headlines
and Get Clients

By Gail Z. Martin

CAREER
PRESS

Pompton Plains, NJ

30 DAYS TO ONLINE PR & MARKETING SUCCESS
Edited And Typeset By Diana Ghazzawi
Original cover design by Wes Youssi
Updated by Jeff Piasky
Printed in the U.S.A.

To order this title, please call toll-free 1-800-CAREER-1 (NJ and Canada: 201-848-0310) to order using VISA or MasterCard, or for further information on books from Career Press.

The Career Press, Inc.
220 West Parkway, Unit 12
Pompton Plains, NJ 07444
www.careerpress.com

Library of Congress Cataloging-in-Publication Data
Martin, Gail Z., 1962-
   30 days to online PR & marketing success : the 30 day results guide to making the most of Twitter, Facebook, Linkedin, and blogging to grab headlines and get clients / by Gail Martin.
       p. cm.
   Includes index.
   ISBN 978-1-60163-180-0 -- ISBN 978-1-60163-646-1 (ebook)
       1. Internet marketing. 2. Public relations. 3. Online social networks. 4. Social media. I. Title. II. Title: Thirty days to online PR & marketing success.

HF5415.1265.M3289 2012
658.8'72--dc23

                                                                2011036946

This book is dedicated to heroic small business owners who gain new skills every day to promote their companies and better serve their clients.

~~~

It takes a village to create a book. Thanks first of all to my husband, Larry, and my three children, Kyrie, Chandler, and Cody. They graciously support my writing, and cope with the travel required by speaking engagements based on the books. Thanks also to the amazing crew at Career Press for excellent editing and production. And of course, thanks also to my agent, John Willig, and to Randy Peyser at AuthorOneStop, who helped to make the connection.

Contents

Author's Note

A word about the way this book works: If you read *30 Days to Social Media Success* or other books in this series, you may find the first six chapters to be familiar. That's because they lay the groundwork for the rest of the advice in the book. If you're a new reader, these chapters are essential to get the maximum value from the book. If you're a returning reader, feel free to review these chapters so that the information is fresh in your mind; you'll need it going forward.

~~~

Though the author and editors have used their best efforts in preparing this book, they make no representations or warranties with respect to the accuracy, fitness, applicability, or completeness of the contents of this book, and specifically disclaim any implied warranties, merchantability, or fitness for a particular purpose. No warranty may be created or extended by sales representatives or written sales materials. The advice and strategies contained herein may not be suitable for your situation. You should consult with a professional where appropriate. Neither the editor nor authors shall be liable for any loss of profit or any commercial damages, including but not limited to special, incidental, direct, indirect, punitive, consequential, or other damages arising directly or indirectly from any mentioned product, service, or Website, or from the use of this material, which is provided "as is." Nothing in this book should be construed as a guarantee of results or earnings. Your results depend on many factors, including your effort and skill. No warranty is made by either the author or the publisher for the performance, effectiveness, or applicability of any sites listed or linked to in this book. The Websites cited in the book and all associated trademarks are the property of their rightful owners. Neither the author nor the publisher control the content on any third-party sites mentioned in the book, and no warranty or guarantee of results is made regarding the products or services offered by third-party sites mentioned in the book. All brand names are the property of their rightful owners.

Foreword

There is some really good news today for small businesses and solo professionals: online marketing and public relations (PR) have changed the way the promotion game is played, and it's leveled the playing field for small organizations. Just think, before the advent of the Internet, even local marketing required a fairly large budget for postage, printing, and advertising. And forget about trying to compete with bigger companies, because it was nearly impossible for a small, local company to extend its reach beyond its immediate community.

Thanks to the Internet, small businesses and organizations now have access to tools and resources that not only let them look as professional as the "big guys," but are easy to use and, even more important for small businesses, incredibly affordable. The Internet has made do-it-yourself, template-driven tools, such as Constant Contact's e-mail marketing, social media marketing, event marketing, and online survey tools, possible. These tools give small businesses the power to not only build strong relationships with current customers but also drive those oh-so-important word-of-mouth recommendations that bring new customers to the table. Furthermore, the Internet has opened global markets for local companies and enabled entrepreneurs to reach larger markets than ever before.

Engaging the customer to build relationships remains at the heart of good online marketing for two simple reasons. First, consumers like to do business with people they've gotten to know. Second, we're a recommendation-based society, and today, getting recommendations from friends, friends of friends, and total strangers is as easy as the click of a button via social networks and ratings/review sites. Online marketing tools make it easy for companies to engage with customers, build relationships, promote their brand, increase their visibility, and position themselves for success.

Here at Constant Contact, we work with more than 450,000 small businesses and organizations, so if there is one thing we know, it's what small businesses need. I can tell you that Gail Martin has her finger on the small-business pulse. I love *30 Days to Online Marketing and PR Success*, because it clearly articulates what small businesses need to know to grasp essential Internet marketing ideas and quickly put them into action. It shows you how to incorporate techniques such as e-mail marketing with other tools, such as social media marketing, mobile advertising, online PR, and search engine optimization, to help your organization succeed. If you want a step-by-step guide to getting started with online marketing, this is the book for you.

—Nancie Freitas
Chief Marketing Officer
Constant Contact, Inc.

Why Most PR and Marketing Fails

1

Marketing horror stories. You've probably heard them. You may have one yourself. These are the stories about how someone tried a marketing technique, sent out a press release, or ran an ad, and "it didn't work."

I've heard plenty of these stories. And as with most urban legends, there's usually more to the story than meets the eye. If you're reading this book, you're a coach, consultant, speaker, author, or owner of a small business, and you want more from your marketing than you're currently getting. You may not be marketing at all because your business is new, or because you're afraid to fail. Or it may be that your marketing is chugging along with mediocre returns or muddled measurement.

Take heart. Marketing isn't mysterious, and once you understand how the pieces fit together, you'll be in a better position to market your own company or to oversee someone to handle marketing for you. Let's start by looking at the seven most common reasons that marketing plans fail.

1. No planning. Many marketing efforts fail because there is no link between the marketing actions and the bottom-line business plan goals that drive revenue. Decision makers get caught up with a vivid, creative idea that isn't accountable to the bottom line, or because they take a "great deal" offered by a salesperson for a media buy. Marketing without a plan is a disaster waiting to happen.

2. Inappropriate actions. If there is no plan, then marketing actions may conflict with each other. It's unlikely that scatter-shot actions will support a business plan goal. Disappointing results come about because of a "ready, fire, aim" approach where actions aren't anchored to business objectives and target audiences. Attempts to copy what a successful competitor is doing without understanding why (or whether) the action is working for them is also a dangerous approach.

3. Lack of clarity about the target market. Blasting out marketing without a clear target is wasteful and unsuccessful. You can't hit a target if you haven't identified it. There is a "sweet spot" of potential customers who could become your ideal clients. You'll need to get to know them to win them.

4. Lack of clear goals. Not only do your marketing actions need to be linked to specific business goals, but each marketing action should be measurable. Build in measurability up front so expectations are clear.

5. Unreasonable expectations. Many people become disillusioned with marketing because they don't understand the benchmarks for successful programs. For example, most direct mail professionals are thrilled to get a 1-percent response rate. One percent! Yet many small businesses send out a postcard mailing and quit in disgust, expecting a response of 20 percent, 30 percent or more. It's important to have realistic expectations so you recognize success when you see it.

6. Unclear on how marketing works. For many people, marketing is a lot like a DVD player. They don't know (and

don't care) how it works. Your odds of creating successful marketing are slim without some knowledge of how the pieces function and the process required to pull the pieces together. On the Internet, new tools are emerging almost daily. Understanding what makes marketing tick is essential whether you're doing it yourself or delegating it to someone else.

7. Lack of patience. Did you know that marketing research shows that it takes between seven to 30 "touches" to make a sale? Customers won't buy until they have an urgent need. Until then, all you can do is create name recognition and a good reputation. That's the value of the Rule of 30. Marketing has a lot in common with farming. You wouldn't plant seeds one day and go out the next and dig them up in disgust because full grown plants hadn't sprouted overnight. Seeds take time to sprout. Marketing seeds also take time to grow.

Putting the 30 Day Guide to Use

Marketing success begins with RESULTS. The **RESULTS** approach stands for:

Recommit to marketing.

Expect success.

Seek partners.

Understand your audience.

Look for win-win scenarios.

Take strategic action.

Stay visible.

In the next 30 days, you can see your social media marketing go from zero to zoom by applying the **RESULTS** formula.

Recommit to set aside at least 30 minutes each day to developing your social media marketing strategy for the next 30 days. (Thirty minutes is a minimum. Once you get started, you'll want to spend an hour, so block out the time now.)

Expect success by throwing yourself whole-heartedly into this 30-day commitment. If the little voice in the back of your head keeps saying, "This is ridiculous. This isn't going to work," you are programming yourself for failure. Program yourself for success by writing down 30 things you would like to achieve from your online marketing and PR strategy. Some ideas include:

~ Reach new ideal prospects who may not know about your product/service and give them an incentive to learn more.

~ Gain visibility in local, regional, national and professional media.

~ Position your company as the expert and leader in its field.

Considering these three examples, come up with your own list of 30 Success Expectations and keep them handy to check back on.

Seek partners. Success in the online world is just as dependent on partnership and collaboration as in the "real" world. These partners might be trusted vendors on whom you rely for your online marketing tools, ecommerce applications, or PR distribution. They might also be companies in non-competing fields that serve the same customer base with whom you can create products and joint ventures.

Understand your audience in more profitable detail than ever before with the exercises in Chapter 3. Make a list of 30 things you wished you knew about your best customers—and create 30 questions you can use for quizzes, surveys and online discussions.

Look for win-win scenarios. When you select among online PR opportunities, be sure the sites you pick are frequently used by reporters, bloggers, and others in the media.

Take strategic action by putting what you learn in this book to work for you. Be sure to do the exercises at the end of each chapter. Complete all 30 chapter exercises in the next 30 days and watch your online marketing and PR soar!

Stay visible by keeping your name in the press through online PR. Create a list of 30 upcoming events, newsworthy items or announcements you could promote with online PR.

Most people put off doing marketing because they think it's too difficult or too time-consuming. By using the principles in this book, you'll do more in 30 minutes a day for 30 days than most business owners do all year. That's the "Get Results" secret weapon—strategic, consistent effort in pursuit of clear, measurable results.

Results Reminder

Planning + Effort +
Consistency = Results

The Rule of 30

How many times are your messages "touching" prospects prior to making the sale? How close is that number to 30?

30

Exercises

1. Describe your primary target audience in detail: age, gender, education, location, income, key concerns, hobbies, aspirations, etc.

2. Justify why this is your primary audience. Now identify your secondary audience and explain why it's in second place. Look at your answers. Are they consistent with your ideal customer? With your current customers? How are they alike and different?

2

The Most Powerful Online PR and Marketing Tool: The Business Plan

If the idea of creating a business plan makes your eyes glaze over, don't worry. This chapter isn't about the kind of detailed business plan you'd need to get a loan from a bank or money from a venture capitalist. In fact, the kind of business plan I'm going to show you just might be the most dynamic document you've ever created, and it is likely to be the most profitable.

If you've already written a business plan, dust it off and take a look at it. If it's more than two years old, its shelf life has expired. Why? Consumer expectations are constantly changing in response to economic conditions, new technology, and lifestyle shifts. So be prepared to make some changes in your approach to assure that it's up to date.

If you've never written a business plan, you're about to find out how to make it your most powerful marketing tool. Pull out a pad of paper and a pen and let's get started.

Define Success in Your Own Terms

Start off by defining what you mean by "success" for the next 12 months. Success can mean different things to different people. Your definition should be what will satisfy you, and it's likely to evolve through time. But unless you know what your success target is for the immediate future, you won't know when you've hit the mark.

Here are some ways to define business success for any given year:

~ Profit.

~ Market share.

~ New product penetration.

~ Media coverage and endorsements.

~ National distribution channels.

~ Percent gain in product sales.

~ Industry credibility—speaking engagements, interviews, board or committee roles.

You may think of a few more possibilities. Success is more than just money, although for most companies and solo professionals, there is a target amount of money involved.

Ready, Aim...

Now write down your top three business goals for next year. Be sure to prioritize them. Do they match your definition of success?

One of the reasons marketing often fails for small businesses and solo professionals is that the marketing is not aligned with the prioritized business plan goals. Overwhelmed business owners take whatever marketing opportunities cross their paths, or buy into "deals" offered to them by persuasive media salespeople. They don't know how to say yes with confidence and no without guilt, because they don't have any standard to judge the opportunities.

Your business plan sets that standard. Next to each of your prioritized business goals, write down who the target audience is for that goal. The more precisely you can narrow down the target audience (instead of "everyone" it would be better to say "college-educated men between the ages of 18–30"), the more precisely you'll be able to target your marketing. You may have more than one target audience for each goal (for now), or you may have the same target audience for all of your goals. That's okay. We'll look at your audiences in more detail in the next chapter.

...Fire! Or Aim Again

Once you've matched an audience with a prioritized goal, make a list of all your current marketing efforts. List everything: Website, banner ads, Facebook ads, online marketing efforts, direct mail, print or radio ads, signage, social media, e-mail newsletters, speaking appearances, online and traditional press release distribution, etc.

Now that you've made a comprehensive list, match each marketing effort to the target audience it reaches, and to the business goal it supports. Do you see any disconnects?

Usually at this point, business owners notice that they have marketing that aren't communicating a message that supports the business goal that is now linked to that audience. Sometimes, business owners discover "orphan" marketing efforts that don't seem to connect with any prioritized business goal. Orphan marketing efforts might exist out of habit, or because they met an old need, or because there's an emotional connection to the action or to the person who sold it to you. But if it's not advancing a business goal, it's an "orphan" because there is no reason to keep on doing it. They might also find marketing that is communicating the right message for a goal, but to the wrong audience.

Getting the message in sync with the best target audience in support of the right prioritized goal is the first step to marketing success. Online marketing and PR will be most successful if the content or offer are linked to the right goal and audience, and you'll get a multiplier effect on all of your marketing activities if they are all in sync. Good online marketing and PR not only help to raise your company's visibility, they also drive prospective clients to your Website and develop brand recognition. If those marketing actions aren't tied to the right goals and audiences, your prospect will get a muddled, ineffective message that will cost you sales.

Look for Gaps

Now it's time to go "gap hunting." Here are questions to ask yourself when you gap hunt:

~ Are there any goals/audiences without any supporting marketing efforts?

~ Are all the marketing efforts bunched up around one goal?

~ Is most of your marketing effort supporting your top prioritized goal?

~ Are you putting most of your effort into goals you've ranked as second or third in importance?

~ Do you have target audiences who aren't the focus of any marketing?

~ Is one target audience getting all the marketing messages?

~ Are second- or third-goal audiences getting more marketing messages than your top goal audience?

Make a list of these marketing gaps, because you'll need to address them in your strategy, and you'll want to look for ways online marketing and PR can help you plug the holes.

Defining Your Transformative Value

Before any customer spends money, he or she has to overcome two obstacles: ego and money. Ego is what makes people try to fix a problem themselves, rather than hire someone. They don't agree to buy until they fail. Money is what clients hope to save by doing the job themselves. Most people won't hire someone for any job until 1) they have failed to do it themselves, and 2) there is enough at stake that continued failure will cost more than paying for the job.

Every person who buys your product does so because he or she has a problem. For example, if you are a business coach who specializes in work/life balance, your clients set aside time and money to work with you because their current balance isn't functioning well. If you run a roofing firm, clients hire you to replace missing shingles. "Balance" or "missing shingles" are the problem.

Behind the problem is a pain. That's the chance that the problem could get bigger. The work/life balance issue could begin to impact a person's relationships, or the ability to complete projects. A few missing shingles could lead to water damage and more expensive repairs.

Underneath the pain is a fear. The fear is the "what if" that keeps a prospect up at night envisioning the worst scenario. The work/life balance issue could lead to a divorce, delinquent children, bankruptcy. Water damage could mean expensive structural damage.

Your Transformative Value is the way you speak to the problem/pain/fear in your own unique way. When you make a sale, it's because you have done two things: Successfully answered the ego/money challenge and satisfied the problem/pain/fear issue. To satisfy the ego/money challenge, you've convinced the prospect that you have skills they don't in order to save them money with better results. You've resolved the problem/pain/fear issue by assuring them that you can fix the initial problem so well that the pain and fear disappear.

Successful marketing communicates your unique Transformative Value to your best prospects to satisfy both the Ego/Money objection and to solve the Problem/Pain/Fear. Online marketing and PR are two of the channels you can use to communicate that message effectively.

Results Reminder

Invest most of your marketing effort into achieving your number-one business goal.

The Rule of 30

Can you identify 30 ways your marketing speaks to your Transformative Value?

30

Exercises

1. Prioritize your top three business goals.
2. Match them to their target audience.
3. Match the marketing to the goals/audience and gap hunt.
4. Determine the Transformative Value for each goal/audience.

3

Digging Into the Business Plan for a PR and Marketing Payoff

Let's spend a little more time talking about your target audiences before we move on, because the key to all marketing is to give the right message to the right person. Matching the message to the target audience is still essential in online marketing and PR, even though it may seem as if your information is reaching everyone on the Internet.

In marketing, it's easier and more cost efficient to go where your best target audience is already congregating, rather than trying to get them to form a new group. That's the thinking behind magazine, TV, and radio sales people who show you a media kit that details who reads, watches, or listens to their product. The same thinking is true of events and social media sites. You'll get more exposure for your money if you address a group that already exists rather than spending time and effort to build a brand new group and attract people to it.

Unfortunately, most small businesses and solo professionals have been so busy handling whatever business comes in the door that they haven't stopped to really think about who their best customers are. Even fewer have thought about who their customers *should be* in order to achieve their business goals.

Getting to Know All About You

In Chapter 1, you wrote down a lot of details about your target audience(s). Take out that list, and compare it to the goal/audience/marketing notes you made in Chapter 2.

Here are some questions to ask:

~ Does your original audience profile match your new goal/audience/marketing notes?

~ Are there second-level or third-level audiences you need to describe?

~ How well do the target audiences you have described match your current core customers? What are the similarities? What are the differences?

Now think about those prioritized business goals again. Your number-one business goal should reflect your definition for success this year. Is your current core customer likely to help you achieve your business goal?

Let me give you an example. Suppose you're a life coach, someone who helps people clarify their vision of success for their business or career. Right now, your calendar is full of people who coach with you for one or two one-hour sessions and then move on. Very few of them return as clients after their initial sessions. They like you and appreciate the results, but they say money is the reason they stop after just a few sessions.

Now suppose you have as your top business goal to take your clients further through a new five-week coaching program. You would like to charge more for the program than you do for the regular coaching sessions, and your goal factors in two desirable outcomes: 1) making more income from the same amount of time, and 2) locking in a longer income stream.

As happy as you've been with your current core customers, and as pleased as they've been with your work, it's not likely that they will be the best target audience for your new program. Why? It's probably out of their price range. That means you'll need to identify a new target audience for your business goal that is interested in what you have to offer and that can pay your increased price.

You also need to think about the clients you currently have who don't fit any of your business-goal target audiences. Maybe they were among your first clients when you started your business, and your vision has changed as time moved on. Perhaps you took whoever walked in the door. Maybe some of them haven't been pleasant or profitable, or maybe the work you're doing for them no longer fits with your goals. You'll want to take a good look at their characteristics to avoid attracting more problem clients, and you certainly don't want to make them a target audience. It's your call as to whether you gently let the current misfit clients know that you can no longer serve their needs or whether you just let them gradually drift away, but it's just as helpful to be clear about who you *don't* want as it is to know specifically who you *do* want.

For any of your marketing to work at peak effectiveness, it needs to focus not just on an audience that *could* buy your product, but on the audience that is the *absolute best match* for your product. There will always be some less-than-perfect clients who slip in around the edges, but you don't want to market to them. You want to market to your best customer.

People who were your best customer when you started out may not still be a good fit as your company grows and your goals change. That's okay. It's part of the lifecycle of a business. You will save yourself time, energy, and money by knowing as much as you can about your best customer so that your message will be on-target to solve their Problem/Pain/Fear. One of the scariest things for business owners is to shift their marketing from an original target audience that met their needs when they were a start-up to a more precisely targeted audience that meets their goals today. But unless you change your audience to suit your goals, your marketing is doomed to failure. Your outgrown audience just won't be able to meet your business needs, because your needs aren't in sync with their needs any more.

Make the shift by thinking about the qualities your new best target audience would have, their goals, their visions, and their pain/problem/fear. What will get them past the ego/money wall? Now start to think about where those new audience members are already congregating. What kind of events are they going to? What clubs or associations do they belong to? What social media sites would attract them? What Websites do they visit frequently, where they might see a banner ad? How often do they search for the products and services you provide online, where they might see sponsored search results? Are they getting their information online or through traditional media? What media are they reading? Now is a good time to update your goals/target audiences with what you've just learned.

SWOT the Competition

When you first started your company, you probably focused on what you did best that people would pay for, and you may not have thought much about the competition. Let's start now. Think about the other companies you've encountered who provide products or services similar to yours. They could be local, regional or national. The scope is determined by where your prospects are looking to find solutions more than it is by whether or not you consider yourself to be a regional or national company.

Here are some things to consider:

- ~ How many other companies provide a similar service locally?
- ~ How far will my prospects drive to obtain what I sell?
- ~ Can my prospects get what they need online or over the phone? (If so, you're competing regionally and nationally.)
- ~ What's similar/different about my product/service/delivery than what my competitors offer?
- ~ How are the companies I admire providing the types of products/services I'd like to provide a few years from now?

~ How are other companies offering value and convenience?

~ How do my materials or Website compare in professionalism to competitors?

~ What's special about the things I offer or the way I do business to make my target prospect pick me over someone else?

Now that you've put your thinking cap on, it's time to make some notes. Take a piece of paper and divide it into four equal boxes. Mark the boxes "Strengths," "Weaknesses," "Opportunities" and "Threats." Now fill in the boxes from what you've just learned.

As you focus your marketing message, you'll want to emphasize your unique strengths (which includes your Transformational Value) and go after opportunities (including your new best customers or overlooked pockets of customers who need what you have to sell). At the same time, you will need to be aware of your weaknesses and watch out for threats.

Remember when I told you that everyone has a different definition for success? It's true about Weaknesses and Threats, too. One Weakness of your business may be that competitors sell at a lower price. But if your price is justified by superior craftsmanship or materials, you could turn that Weakness into a Strength that becomes a Threat to your competitor's lower quality product.

Threats, also, are a matter of perspective. If you are a personal trainer, you might think that every other personal trainer in town is a Threat. However, the truth is that many of those trainers aren't going after your target customer because they're chasing a different target that fits their different goals. For example, if you specialize in helping women stay active during and after pregnancy, and another trainer specializes in training busy female executives, you might turn that Threat into a great two-way referral source as you refer clients back and forth to each other as the clients go on maternity leave and return to the workplace.

Results Reminder

Know your competitors and your best customers as well as you know yourself.

The Rule of 30

What are 30 characteristics of the prospects who best fit your number-one goal?

30

Exercises

1. Reassess your core customers in light of your prioritized business goals.

2. Update your target audiences to be the best prospects for achieving your new goals.

3. Now that you know your SWOT, look for hidden Opportunities and Strengths. For example, a high-integrity competitor might become a partner for collaboration, which turns a former Threat into an ally.

Mining PR and Marketing Gems From the Business Plan

4

Now that you're clear on your goals, priorities, target audience, and SWOT, it's time to talk about money.

Budgeting Time and Money

Successful marketing takes either cash or a "cash equivalent." A "cash equivalent" is what you use instead of cash. That could be time that you barter, but more often than not, it's old-fashioned elbow grease. Marketing requires time, and it also requires some money. If you have more time, you can save money. If you have less time, you can get the same work done by hiring help. One way or another, good marketing is going to require investment.

I've heard business owners say that they had such a great location or product that they could "do business by accident." And I've driven past their location when it went up for sale after they went out of business. Success happens because of hard work, strategy, and, yes, a little optimized luck. It doesn't happen by accident.

What do I mean by "optimized luck"? Optimized luck is what happens when you've done your homework, worked as hard as you can, and a great opportunity opens up in front of you. If you hadn't prepared yourself, you wouldn't be ready to make the most of the opportunity, or you might not even notice it. But you also didn't just get lucky. You prepared and trained so that you'd recognize luck when it showed up, and so you would be ready to maximize your big break. It's definitely not "doing business by accident."

Take another look at your prioritized goals/target audiences/ current marketing actions. If you've made a table, add another column for cost. Write down what you think your current marketing actions are costing you. The cost could be in time, or it could be in real money. It could be the cost of hiring someone to update your Website or design your brochure, or it could include printing, postage, advertising, or other fees. You could include membership dues for the groups you've joined to mingle with your target audience. Make the best estimates you can and then look at the results.

Here are a few questions to ask yourself:

~ How much are you currently spending for each goal?

~ Are you spending the most to achieve your top goal?

~ Is what you're spending worth the potential new revenue that goal could provide?

~ Could you spend more if it would achieve your goal faster?

If you are spending more to achieve your third priority than you are for your top priority, you've got a problem. If you're spending more to achieve a goal with smaller revenue potential than for a goal with larger revenue potential, it's time to reconsider. If you're not spending anything, hoping to do business by accident, then you're on thin ice.

Online marketing becomes much more cost effective when it targets a highly defined audience. Your online PR efforts will also have more success when you know your audience well enough to provide news and information they want and need. By focusing, you'll stop wasting time and money on efforts that aren't reaching your ideal prospects effectively. Your highly targeted, strategic online marketing and PR efforts will be more successful because you'll be giving your prospects what they need. You gain by converting more prospects into customers while spending time and money more effectively.

How Much is Enough?

I've seen all kinds of estimates on how much a marketing budget should be. An industry standard is 5 percent of revenue. I've seen companies spend far less and far more than 5 percent and get results that met their definition of success. What matters most is that you spend your budget wisely.

A zero budget won't keep you in business long, and it certainly won't help you grow. If you truly have no cash, you'll need to roll up your sleeves and put sweat equity to work. If this describes your situation, how many hours can you put into doing marketing? Write it down, and put a dollar estimate of your hourly rate next to it. That's what you're really spending.

If you're already spending money and you're comfortable with that level of investment, be sure that you've prioritized your budget in line with your goals. Put the biggest chunk of money where you'll get the best return or achieve the biggest goal.

If you're willing to invest more, then determine a dollar amount you can spend and divide it among your prioritized goals. Budgeting money doesn't obligate you to spend it, but it does give you a tool to prioritize new opportunities, and it may free you to investigate options you might not have considered.

Setting a budget also creates one way to measure effectiveness. Over time, you'll want to ask yourself whether a particular marketing method is earning its keep. Knowing what you've budgeted for it compared to its value can help you decide what to keep and what to change.

The Irresistible Difference

Before we leave the nitty-gritty of your business plan, there's one item left we need to talk about, your "Irresistible Difference."

You already know your Transformational Value. That's how you address your prospect's Problem/Pain/Fear and overcome his Ego/Money objection. Your Irresistible Difference is what draws a prospect to you and your company as opposed to your competitors.

Your Irresistible Difference should tap directly into who your best prospect/customer is. It should fit that customer like their favorite pair of jeans, not only covering what's necessary, but making them feel wonderful as well.

Go back to your best customer's qualities. What can you provide in your service, package, or delivery that will meet their need as well as their unspoken desire? For some customers, convenience is king. For others, it's value, or reliability, or exceptional knowledge. Not only will you gain some good insights into powerful marketing copy by looking for the Irresistible Difference, but you'll also get some great ideas for where to find your best prospects and how to reach them.

For example, customers who prize value may join online communities dedicated to saving money. Those could be great places for you to participate through chat, forum posts and blogs because your audience is already there. A brand-conscious customer may place more value in being a member of professional and alumni associations and participating at a higher-than-average level. You might find those groups particularly useful to your marketing strategy because they tap into qualities the prospect prizes.

Your Irresistible Difference demonstrates how well you understand the quality the prospect values through where you market (including your choice of online marketing, social media, and PR), how you structure your product/service, how you deliver your product, and how you position your company in the marketplace.

As you become aware of the Irresistible Difference you offer to your different target audiences, make a note of it so you won't forget to put its power to work for you.

Results Reminder

Effective marketing isn't free. Prioritize your money and sweat equity and make it count.

The Rule of 30

What are 30 different ways you could illustrate your Irresistible Difference to your prospects and customers?

30

Exercises

1. Determine your marketing budget for each prioritized business goal. Be sure the biggest budget supports the top goal.

2. Figure out what you can really spend on marketing this year in time and money. Split that among your prioritized goals.

3. Identify your Irresistible Difference and start thinking about where your best prospects are already congregating.

Creating a PR and Marketing Action Plan

5

Now you're ready to create an action plan. Your action plan is the key to the rest of your 30-day success because it's your compass and checklist.

Your action plan takes all the pieces you've put together so far and creates a way for you to make them happen. You won't achieve every item on your action plan in 30 days, but you can lay the groundwork to achieve them, and make real progress toward your goal.

To be successful, your action plan needs to be detailed. Vague goals such as "I want to bring in more business" are not helpful, because they lack the detail to enable you to take action toward making the goal a reality.

Action plan items must also advance at least one business plan goal by addressing that goal's target audience. You've already attached marketing actions to each goal/audience. This is a good time to look at those marketing actions and break them into smaller steps. That will give you a better idea of the time and money—and specific actions—necessary to make them happen.

For example, perhaps your top business plan goal is to get more visibility about your products and services. You've identified the target audience, and you've decided to use the Internet to reach them. That's a step in the right direction, but not enough to really get you going.

Let's break "use online marketing and PR" into several action steps.

~ Identify the Websites, blogs, and online news and entertainment channels that your ideal prospect is already reading. These may be good for your PR announcements.

~ Understand what circumstances or events trigger your customer to make a purchase. For example, if your customer values product reviews, it makes sense to put effort into getting your product reviewed by a reputable Website.

~ Determine what kinds of social media and smart phone applications your customer is already using. How much do they use the Internet and devices such as cell phones in their daily routine?

~ Build on the e-mail list of your current opt-in customers. What can you offer new prospects to encourage them to opt-in to your newsletter list?

~ Take a look at your ability to process transactions online. Do you have an online shopping cart and does it give you room to grow?

~ Think about how you are currently promoting your events, special offers, and other news. Are you taking full advantage of new online media?

Do you see how action steps take your marketing from being a great idea to something tangible? As you read through the rest of the chapters in the book, don't just write down marketing ideas, turn those ideas into step-by-step action plans and attach them to the appropriate prioritized business goal and its target audience. This one step will make an amazing difference in the results you see from your online marketing and PR, because it will make it clear what you can do every day to make your goals happen.

Results Reminder

If a goal or a marketing strategy seems too daunting, break it down into action steps and then tackle one step at a time in sequential order to make it happen!

The Rule of 30

Your daily 30 minutes for marketing should always advance or achieve one of your top priority action plan items.

30

Exercise

Take a fresh look at the marketing actions you identified. Can you break each marketing action into at least three to five action plan steps that could be handled in 30 minutes a day?

6 Finding Your Real Story and True Voice

Have you ever noticed how some companies seem to change who they are and how they sound with each new marketing campaign? Even worse, have you ever seen a company portray a totally different personality depending on whether you go to their Website, read a brochure, see them at a trade show or hear one of their commercials?

Many companies have a mish-mash of marketing materials that have been created over time, often by many different people. Some companies seem to lurch from strategy to strategy, never investing the time to allow any single approach to take root and pay off. Customers become confused, because the company doesn't seem to know its own identity. Even worse, a company that seems to change its personality every month can seem insincere, even untrustworthy.

The Internet complicates this disconnect because it's easier than ever for prospects to hop from site to site, and if your company's personality seems to change between your

Website, blog, online brochure, articles and social media sites, your prospect will start to wonder who the "real" you is. Customers know when the tone of your online marketing doesn't match the rest of their experience with your firm, or when the PR isn't consistent with what they see on your Website.

One of the easiest ways to fix this is to discover the Real Story of your company, and the True Voice that is uniquely yours.

Telling Your Real Story

Remember the problem/pain/fear that drives your prospect past ego and money objections to seek out help? Your Real Story should demonstrate how you have solved a very similar problem/pain/fear for someone else, someone to whom the reader can relate.

The story format is especially powerful for sharing this information because human beings, even in the Internet age, are hard-wired to listen to stories. Stories sell.

Use your Real Story as a way to make an emotional connection with readers and to differentiate your firm from others in the same industry. It should create a personality that is unique to your company.

What is the story of your business? Here are five ways to uncover your Real Story:

~ The owner's story. Some types of stories reach very deep into the American consciousness. Stories about second chances, self-made successes, hard-working newcomers who realize the American dream and reinvention speak to very deeply held beliefs about who we are. I knew a business owner who came to the U.S. as an exchange student from China, received her education and met her husband here. Because of the gift of a pearl necklace from an aunt back in China who knew a pearl farmer, this woman and her husband now own a pearl importing and jewelry design business. Her story of reinvention while retaining her roots has gotten positive media coverage for her business.

~   The product's story. What need does your product meet? The owner of a chain of coin-operated laundries realized that he doesn't just give people clean clothes—he helps them show their love for their families and succeed in the workplace by having a neat and clean appearance. In his city neighborhood of recent immigrants who are climbing the ladder of prosperity, family and self-respect are very deeply held values. Do your services or products offer people security, good health, or a chance to succeed? What is the need that prompts your customer to buy?

~   The business's story. Has your business overcome adversity? We cheer for the businesses that found a way to come back after 9/11 in New York City or after Hurricane Katrina in New Orleans. Has your company weathered bad times, lopsided competition, succession crises or problems, and come back stronger than ever? People love a come-back story.

~   Your customers' stories. Go beyond testimonials. A case study tells the story of the problem and how your company solved it—but it's really a story about a hero, a dragon and a damsel in distress. The dragon is the business problem—for example, a project badly behind schedule and over budget. Your company is the hero. The client is the damsel in distress. Every good adventure has a few plot twists to keep our interest—what challenges happened on the way to slaying the dragon? Did you lose key project personnel when you needed them most? Did a piece of crucial equipment break or get delayed in shipping? Details like this make your story compelling. And then there's the happy ending—how your company solved the problem and what it meant for the customer—significant dollar savings, productivity enhancement, the ability to compete in new markets. Help listeners feel the real benefit.

~ The story of your mission. Is your company part of your mission in life? Do you want to make the world a better place through the product or service you provide? Perhaps you became a lawyer because someone in your family was taken advantage of, and you want to make sure that others receive justice. Maybe you learned martial arts because you were robbed and ended up opening a studio to teach others to be safe. Your mission goes beyond your personal story to make a difference in the world around you. Even the most mundane business can have a mission. Maybe you repair cars, but your commitment is to keep people from being endangered by breakdowns or from losing their jobs because of unreliable transportation. How do you make a difference?

Telling the Real Story of your business makes a powerful connection with potential customers. It can be the springboard to compelling media coverage. It can differentiate you from competitors. Once you uncover your Real Story, it affects the way you communicate about your business and the way you think about yourself, your products and your customers.

The Power of Your True Voice

Many people put off marketing their companies because they don't feel authentic when they are in sales mode, or they believe that marketing is inherently untruthful. How would you feel about doing marketing for your business if it felt completely authentic? Would you be able to overcome childhood instructions not to boast if the words seemed natural, honest, and comfortable?

Using your True Voice to market your firm feels natural and sounds authentic. The True Voice of your business are the words that show up again and again in the way you and others describe your company. Many companies never recognize their True Voice, so their marketing materials sound contrived, generic, or insincere.

Here are four tips to find and use the True Voice of your business:

1. Listen to yourself. The next time someone asks you to tell them about your company, listen to yourself as you talk. If you have developed an "elevator speech," write it down and take a good look. What verbs are you using? What adjectives? What nouns? Make a list; you'll come back to it as you work through the tips.

2. Listen to your clients. Take some of your best clients to lunch and ask them to tell you what they like about your company. Or, pull out the comment cards and e-mails sent by happy customers and look at the words they use. Jot down the nouns, verbs, adjectives, and phrases that show up. Underline the words and phrases that are used frequently.

3. Listen to your employees. Ask your best employees how they help customers. Ask them to describe the business and its products—and the solutions you provide. Add the key words and phrases to your list.

4. Listen to your friends. If you are introduced by one of your colleagues, what words do they use to describe your business and your service? Read over your own marketing materials. Do the same solutions or phrases pop up frequently? Write them down.

You now have a list of key words and phrases that naturally describe what you do, who you serve, and what benefit you provide. To use your True Voice, take the most powerful words from your list use those words and phrases intentionally throughout your spoken and written communications.

When you use these True Voice words and phrases, you will feel honest and comfortable, because the words spring from who you really are and from the mission of your company. You'll find it easy to differentiate your services, because your words describe your strengths and the benefits you provide. Intentionally using the True Voice of your business will make your message unique, compelling, and natural in both your online marketing and in your online and offline PR.

Results Reminder

Your Real Story told in your True Voice is memorable, credible, and compelling.

The Rule of 30

What are 30 different words or phrases that come naturally as you talk about your product, service, and results?

30

Exercises

1. Identify your strongest Real Story. Now brainstorm ways you can share it through the power of PR.

2. Once you've compiled your list of your True Voice words, keep it handy as you develop your press releases, article pitches, and online marketing content.

7 Touches to Transactions

Modern marketing wisdom holds that in today's advertising-saturated world, it takes at least seven to 30 "touches" or reminders before a consumer takes action. Although that may seem like a lot when you first hear it, if you think about how you act when you're the consumer, it begins to make sense.

Your online marketing and PR can account for several of those 30 touches. But to be effective, you need to think about how touches become transactions.

Touches and Trigger Points

We ignore tens of thousands of advertising messages every day, mostly because they promote products we aren't currently interested in buying. The key word there is "currently." When you realize you need a product or service, all of a sudden, you tune into the messages related to the product/service that you had been screening out.

The situation that changes everything is a trigger point. It's an event that moves you from someone who hasn't thought about making a purchase or who has been casually window shopping to someone who needs to buy right now. The seller usually can't change the trigger point (although they try to influence it with education, sales, and specials), but you can make enough touches so that when a triggering event moves a prospect from looker to buyer, he or she thinks about your company.

Let's use a car purchase as an example. If your car is reasonably new and in good working order, you may not be thinking about buying a new car. You probably tune out car ads, emails from dealerships, or radio commercials. Or maybe you've been thinking about buying a new car—some day. You might be casually reading ads, going to dealer Websites, paying some attention to commercials, even slowing down when you pass the dealer's lot for a good look. But for now, it's all still window shopping.

Then a triggering event occurs. Your existing car is in an accident, and it will cost more to fix it than it's worth. All of a sudden, you're in the market for a new car, and you need it right now.

Until that triggering event happened, there wasn't much the car dealers could do to hurry up your purchase. You bought the car based on your schedule of when you needed one, not on the dealer's schedule of when he wanted to sell one. Business owners often forget that it's the customers' need that drives the purchase cycle more than it is driven by sales and specials. But there's a very important thing to remember: when a customer moves from shopper to buyer, the company that has made the most marketing touches is first in line to get his business.

Go back to the car example. When that prospect was window shopping, the dealership with the best Website, or the showroom that was polite about a test drive without a commitment is likely to be the first place that prospect goes when he or she moves from shopper to buyer. Those touches pay off in top-of-mind awareness.

Where does online marketing and PR come in? Well-placed online marketing is a low-pressure way to remain in the forefront of a prospect's awareness with touches on a subject where there's interest but no trigger for an immediate purchase. It can also keep your company in touch with current customers so that when add-ons or upgrades become necessary, you're first in line for the business. Regular, strategic online PR increases your company's visibility and extends your credibility as an expert. Both visibility and credibility are important to future sales, because prospects must remember you and must believe that you provide a quality product or service.

The key here is not to view online marketing and PR as a way to provide a barrage of buy-now messages. Instead, think of how you can engage the prospect in a conversation about whatever product or service you sell, with the immediate focus on offering helpful information related to the problem/pain/fear.

Some great examples of this might include strategically placed online ads on Websites that your ideal prospect uses frequently. If your customer is constantly on-the-go, a well-timed mobile (cell phone) text ad might encourage a convenience purchase or entertainment choice. A great e-newsletter can extend the conversation with a prospect or customer, gather valuable feedback, and educate about the benefits of the products and services you offer. With an autoresponder, you can send a targeted series of follow-up e-mails to draw a new prospect further down your sales funnel. A good online shopping cart can suggest related products, or provide a "thank-you" discount to encourage a future purchase. Press releases distributed online attract media attention and boost search engine hits. Articles, interviews, and product reviews that mention your name in online media (as a result of your PR efforts) increase your visibility and underscore your credibility and expertise.

Once you've established a relationship, you have the chance to educate the prospect about the trigger point. Perhaps the best time to buy a new piece of equipment isn't when the old equipment falls apart. Perhaps there are trade-in or depreciation advantages to buying on a shorter purchase cycle. Maybe you can point out benefits that deal so much better with the problem/pain/fear than the old product that the prospect decides to buy sooner rather than later. You've altered the trigger point through education, and because you have an ongoing relationship, you're likely to be first in line to get the sale.

When someone subscribes to your e-newsletter, blog, Facebook page update, or Twitter feed, they're agreeing to get updates (information) from you on a regular basis. If you share information that speaks to the prospect's needs, every update reminds the prospect about you (a touch) while it provides useful information (deepening your relationship and educating to alter the trigger point). Online marketing and PR makes it easier and less expensive (and less intrusive) than ever before to stay in contact as touches prepare for a trigger.

Results Reminder

Using a "touch" strategy keeps you visible by providing useful information your targeted audience wants and needs without sales pressure.

The Rule of 30

What content can you offer to provide 30 valuable touches?

30

Exercises

1. Your online marketing and PR "touches" can introduce prospects to your Website, Internet shopping cart, e-newsletter, blog, or other sites. How could you use these "touches" to deepen your relationship with prospects?

2. What content can you communicate through online PR and marketing that would increase your credibility and build trust prior to the prospect's triggering event? Is there information you can share to alter the trigger point through education?

The Power of
Online PR

8

Public relations (PR) and marketing are often mentioned in the same breath, but they are very different, yet complementary, disciplines. PR traditionally deals with free publicity, while marketing is the management of paid promotion.

By free publicity, PR professionals generally mean exposure that did not result from paid advertisement in print, or on radio or TV. Free publicity might be an article, a photo, or an interview on radio or TV. The visibility could come as a result of a news tidbit being deemed worthy of interest by the media gatekeepers—editors, reporters, and producers. Paid publicists spend their time getting to know these gatekeepers, learning their tastes and biases, and gaining access. Their goal is to develop relationships so that they can feed a steady stream of information to the gatekeepers. No actual money changes hands, but the endeavor is certainly not "free" in terms of effort, because it requires both research and a lot of in-person networking.

Marketing, on the other hand, focuses on paid promotion, usually in the form of advertisements, direct mail, billboards, newsletters and materials such as brochures and videos. Events—ranging from charity balls to tradeshows—straddle the line between marketing and PR.

For the moment, let's set aside marketing (we'll come back to it in a few chapters) and focus on public relations (PR). It's important for you to have a clear understanding of how PR works in order to get the most benefit from the substantial changes the Internet has created.

What PR Is—and Isn't

To be effective, a PR campaign must have an underlying plan. You've developed your marketing plan in the first section of this book. Dust it off, because you'll need it.

In order to get results from PR, your outreach needs to have: 1) an immediate goal; 2) a specific target audience (both consumers and media gatekeepers); and 3) a timely, newsworthy hook.

The top business goal that you identified in your marketing plan is a good place to begin your PR planning. Now drill a little deeper. What actions are happening in your company to support that goal? Do you have new product launches? Will you be holding special events? Have you won awards or been named to industry councils? Have you hired staff in senior or customer-facing positions? Are you adding new locations or new online capabilities?

Your next question is "Who cares?" That's where your specific target audience comes into play. What segment of the population will care about your announcement? The more specifically you can identify them by demographics (age, economic status, education, geographic location, and so on) and psychographics (how they perceive themselves), the more successfully you will be able to target your message to reach them. Consumers are just part of the equation. You may have many other "interested bystanders," whom I call "stakeholders." These stakeholders have a reason to care about your company, even if they don't buy your product, because your news affects them in some way.

For example, building a new plant will be of interest to the local commercial real estate market and the city's economic development and business community, to publications that cover your industry, and to banks and investors that finance your company. Your suppliers and distributors will be interested, as will the people who live nearby. The media that reaches these stakeholders will be very interested. Successful PR requires you to think about the people who will be affected—pro and con—by your news and to manage the message.

PR is still a game of relationships, although some of the players have changed. "Traditional" (that is, radio, TV, and print) PR is still important, even though the Internet has created new ways to reach consumers. Part of developing a PR campaign lies in finding out what online and offline media is being consumed by your target audiences (and interested bystanders). What magazines (print or online) do they read? Do they get their news from TV, from magazines, or from blogs and online news? What Websites do they visit?

Not that very long ago, print and broadcast media were the only real venues for PR. Today, you can add blogs, social media sites such as Facebook and YouTube, online press distribution sites such as PRNewswire and PR Web, and thousands of Internet-only publications, radio programs, and online video shows. The number of gatekeepers has grown, reducing the power of traditional reporters and editors. But make no mistake—the gatekeepers of the online PR world still have a big stake in making sure their channels don't become cluttered by junk, so you'll have to prove yourself to get past the gate.

That's where the timely, newsworthy "hook" comes in. Editors, bloggers, and radio hosts aren't in business to promote your product—or anyone else's. They exist because they inform and entertain their audiences. They survive by knowing what interests their audience. They are protective of their audience because today's readers and listeners have very short attention spans, and it takes only a few seconds of boredom to make them put down the publication or change the channel.

This means that reporters, bloggers, Website editors and TV/ radio hosts are picky about what news they share with their consumers. There has to be something in it for the reader/listener. Information makes it past the gatekeeper because the audience wants and/or needs to know it.

This is where many companies miss the boat with PR. They are so wrapped up in their own product, event, or roll-out that they mistakenly think everyone cares—or should care. The harsh fact is that people don't care about your news unless it will impact their lives or help them achieve their goals. Gatekeepers know this—and they want the people who send them press releases to understand this fact, too.

This is why demographics must drive your choice of online and offline media. Too many businesses send out their release to everyone, leaving it to the editors to sort out. That approach rapidly creates a negative impression of your company among media gatekeepers, because they dislike being overwhelmed with news that a casual observer could have realized would not be of interest to their audiences. They want to know that you've done your homework, and that you understand what their readers/listeners want. Your news must be informative, and if it can be entertaining, even better. But it must be targeted, or it won't be considered.

After all this, you may be wondering whether PR is worth the effort. The answer is a resounding yes. One timely mention in a national magazine can easily garner your company visibility that would have cost tens of thousands of dollars to replicate with a paid ad. Many small companies can't possibly pay for consistent print, online, radio, or TV coverage. But a cleverly targeted, informational, and entertaining ongoing PR campaign can result in national and international media mentions, exposing your company to millions of potential customers, partners, resource providers, and investors. Successful PR can burnish your business's image, add to its credibility, and position it as a market influencer.

Developing and nurturing relationships with the media can also be a valuable asset. Having friends among bloggers, reporters, and Web mavens can help you to be among the first to hear crucial business intelligence. When you have earned gatekeepers' respect, you may be invited to participate in events, interviews, and other media events to which you might not have had access on your own. Once you have demonstrated that you understand the needs and interests of their audiences, you are likely to find that your well-targeted releases are picked up more often. A word of warning: Relationships don't *guarantee* placement, nor will they ensure that reporters refrain from mentioning negative news about your company if it arises.

Now that you know what PR is—and isn't, you're ready to understand how the Internet changed everything by enabling companies to reach beyond gatekeepers to the ultimate consumers themselves.

Results Reminder

Create a detailed description of your stakeholders. They're the best audience for your news.

The Rule of 30

Who are the editors, hosts, producers, reporters, bloggers who are speaking to your target audiences? Create a list of at least 30 individuals, including name, media outlet, and e-mail address.

30

Exercises

1. Once you have identified your 30 potential online/offline media targets, spend some time reading them. What is their tone? Who else is featured? Look at their "About Us" section, and read their advertising sales profile to get important details about their audience. Are they right for you?

2. If you aren't sure about what your customers are reading, where they spend their time online, and what they watch or listen to, ask! It's easy to do focus groups and e-mail surveys.

Effective PR and Marketing in the Age of Google

9

I mentioned in the Introduction that the Internet had changed everything for marketing and PR. That's true. While traditional media outlets (newspapers, magazines, TV and radio) remain prominent, online media venues grow daily in importance.

During the last few years, many well-established newspapers and magazines have either ceased publication or gone to online-only editions. This is a reflection of many trends, including a slump in advertiser spending, a shift to online media consumption, and the realities surrounding the cost of creating and distributing traditional print media.

The Do-It-Yourself Consumer

We live in a do-it-yourself society. We pump our own gas, scan and bag our own groceries, and serve ourselves at cafeterias. So it should come as no surprise that today's consumers have begun to take a do-it-yourself to media.

53

Today's consumer isn't limited by the choices presented by local radio stations. He or she can listen to hundreds of highly targeted satellite channels, play a CD or plug in a customized playlist on an iPod. TV watchers can choose from more than a thousand cable channels, pop in a DVD, TiVo a show from a few days ago or download video from Netflix. Print consumers can read news online without waiting for the 6 p.m. broadcast or the next morning's paper. Consumers have become accustomed to getting what they want when they want it.

Google (and the other search engines) changed the world by enabling anyone with a computer to search the Internet in the blink of an eye. Consumers today often start with an Internet search for what they want, and look to more traditional media for validation. So a consumer in the market for a product may start with searches on eBay or Amazon to see what's available, and then look at a ratings magazine, ratings Website or user blog to check reliability and satisfaction.

This do-it-yourself approach has created a world where content is highly customized and personalized. No one else has your iPod playlist. You may create a "portal" page for yourself with links to all of your favorite blogs and Websites, creating a customized stream of news, entertainment, and information. Each of the thousands of cable and satellite TV channels reaches an increasingly targeted consumer, far different from in the days when all of America watched one of three broadcast channels. Satellite radio can focus on a single artist or entertainer as well as a segmented style of music, news, or comedy. It has become essential for anyone trying to reach consumers to speak with the same pinpoint segmentation.

Going Around the Gatekeepers

The Internet has given consumers a huge amount of new information, mostly by going around the traditional gatekeepers. The good and bad news about the Internet is that anyone can post information, and the search engines will find it. Unless the person posting is breaking a law, there is no one to keep them from making their information available. Search engines select results based on relevancy, but say nothing about legitimacy. Consumers have access to a wealth of information, but they also increasingly feel the pressure of information overload.

This shift has caused online media and offline media to rethink their relationship beyond being competitors. In reality, they often form a continuum that permits the consumer-researcher to go as deeply into a topic as he or she desires. The Internet has also created a 24/7 market for information of all kinds, fueling a need for a vast amount of content, some of which comes in the form of press releases. At the same time, overwhelmed consumers still value trusted blogs, online magazines, and other "branded" outlets to deliver information that has been verified to some degree and to weed out the junk.

The need for news never ends. In order to stay fresh, blogs, Websites, and online publications (as well as video sites and Internet radio) must continually release new content. The capacity to consume that content far outstrips what any individual or news team can produce alone. Websites, blogs, and online/traditional radio and TV could not possibly fill all their space or hours of programming without press release-generated news and lifestyle information. Reporters, bloggers, and TV and radio hosts use press releases to find story ideas, discover interesting people to interview, and find new products and events to feature. An increasing number of sites, including CNN, encourage readers to upload their own video. Sites such as BlogTalkRadio.com enable anyone to become an Internet radio host and develop programming with a narrowly targeted audience. This creates an unprecedented opportunity for companies that are adept at positioning their information to inform and entertain highly targeted audiences.

The other big shift is that the Internet and the search engines have put the "public" back in public relations. Traditional PR could only reach the public through media gatekeepers. Today's companies can take their message straight to consumers via the Internet, and as we'll see in the next chapter, that requires changes to the traditional format of the press release, PR's workhorse tool. By reaching the public directly, a company can create demand for a product when consumers request it from retailers. Companies can share more product details than magazines or blogs are likely to cover. When coupled with social media and the interactive tools available online, companies have an unprecedented opportunity to get user feedback and satisfy complaints, potentially increasing satisfaction and strengthening their reputation.

It takes a deft touch (and a detailed understanding of your target audience) to create PR campaigns that satisfy both consumers and the media, but it is worth the effort. The Internet blurs the line between reporter and citizen-journalist. Many individual bloggers have huge followings that traditional newspapers and magazines can only envy. Most consumers read and listen to a blend of "professional" news and citizen-journalist offerings, gathering what they need from both. Companies who ignore online PR opportunities presented by blogs, forums, Websites, Web video, and Internet radio do so at their peril. Huge numbers of consumers make the Internet their first stop for information, making it essential for companies to learn how to be part of the flow, or risk being left behind.

Budgeting Time and Money

Pre-Internet, a PR budget was mainly for paper, envelopes, postage, and fancy fliers. Today, most press releases are sent via e-mail, and extra information is posted on a Website and sent via a hyperlink.

PR budgets require a mix of time and money. Time is required to gather the demographic and psychographic information about your customer, as well as to track online and offline media consumption patterns. You'll also need to budget enough time to research the appropriate traditional and new media you want to target—the blogs, Websites, online/offline newspapers and magazines, TV, Web video, and Internet/broadcast radio outlets best suited to reaching your consumer.

Time is also required to put together well-written press releases and to distribute them in a way that reporters will read. (I'll cover more on the details of how to do that in future chapters.) You'll also need to know the media's deadlines, which can range from nearly instantaneous to six months (or more) in advance. Online and offline promotional tools also take time to create, but add significant value in terms of exposure and engagement.

Today's promotional tools may include traditional standards such as posters, signage, brochures, and flyers. Modern companies also recognize that Websites, Web banners, Facebook ads, online contests and give-aways, free downloadable samples, and specialized social media pages are a vital part of PR that reaches the wired consumer.

The good news is that effective online and traditional PR can be done with more elbow grease than cash. Sites like Vistaprint.com enable you to print materials very inexpensively, while e-mail newsletter providers such as Constant Contact make it possible to create your own online direct mail campaign. If you have the internal resources (or are comfortable doing it yourself), it's possible to create your own Websites, downloads, and social media. If that's outside of your comfort zone or beyond your time budget, you'll need to consider budgeting money for assistance, or bartering for skills.

One of the best things about online PR and marketing is the ability to trace visits, clicks, impressions, page openings, and forwards in real time. You're no longer dependent on an expensive clipping service. Instead, free programs such as Google Alerts make it possible for you to find every time your name, keyword, product, or event is mentioned anywhere on the Internet. This makes it very easy to see which media venues are receptive to your information, and where you may need to rethink your approach.

Results Reminder

How might a reporter's interest in your news differ from that of a consumer? How can you adjust your press releases according to whether you're targeting a journalist or a consumer?

The Rule of 30

Find Internet radio programs, blogs, and specialty online magazines that feature the kinds of services or products you offer. Make a list of 30, including contact names, telephone numbers, and e-mail addresses.

30

Exercises

1. Set Google Alerts (a free service) at *http://www.google.com/alerts* to e-mail you whenever your company or product appears anywhere on the Web. See who's already talking about you—they might be open to getting your announcements.

2. Set your Website to track which keywords are most often used by visitors to find your Website. Make a list of them for future use.

Writing the Online Press Release

10

The press release remains the workhorse document of Public Relations. It's the one-page vehicle for conveying news and announcements in a professional and standard format. Yet even the press release has undergone major changes with the advent of online PR, and if you want your news to shine, it's important to be sure your release is positioned for maximum exposure.

Some Things Never Change

Even though press releases are now distributed via e-mail instead of by fax or postal mail, the basic press release structure remains the same. Press releases use the "inverted triangle" format, which makes editing easier. Think of your release as an upside-down triangle, with the most important facts at the top and the information becoming less important the closer it is to the bottom. Editors cut from the bottom up, assured by the inverted triangle format that the really important information is near the top.

Press releases should rarely be longer than one page (never more than two), should use crisp, action verbs, and should avoid "puffery" or sales language that cannot be substantiated by research. (Don't claim that your product is the best or unique unless you've got data to back up your claim.) If you include a quote, make it meaningful and be sure it's from an important spokesperson or leave it out.

The who, what, when, where, and why should be in the first two paragraphs. Your first paragraph should make it clear why the announcement is important, and the headline should be attention-grabbing. Your second paragraph should provide more details and context to explain what is happening and expand on the impact. A quote, if used, should be in the third or fourth paragraph. Use the last few paragraphs to provide more essential details about your news, but kept it brief and include only what is really necessary. The ending paragraph is a "boilerplate" description of your company, its name and stock symbol (if any), and a link to your Website. You may also include a "for more information" contact phone number and e-mail address.

The conventional format for a press release looks like this:

FOR IMMEDIATE RELEASE

CONTACT: (media contact person's name and e-mail/phone)

HEADLINE: Subhead

DATELINE: First paragraph

Second paragraph

Third paragraph, and so on

Boilerplate company information and Website, for more information contact details.

PR professionals often end their press releases with three hash marks "###" or the word "END" in all caps, enclosed by quotation marks. This practice is a carry-over from the old print days, and it makes clear to an editor that the press release is complete. Including one of these markers isn't essential, but it won't hurt, either.

For examples of real-life press releases using this format, check out my News page at *www.GailMartinMarketing.com*.

Press Releases for an Online World

Press releases intended for an online audience require some important changes. Without these, your press release will be difficult to find, meaning that fewer potential customers will see your news.

Use keywords. "Keywords" are the words consumers use to search for a topic, product, or service. Often, these are generic descriptions rather than company, brand, or product names, because the consumer does not know that information. Google Keyword Tool is a free service that helps you find the words and phrases that are most often used to search for products, services, or topics similar to what you are offering. Put in the words you usually use to describe your product, and Google Keyword Tool will provide a list of alternatives, ranked by how many times users choose that word/ phrase for a search. You'll find that some synonymous words vary tremendously in popularity. If two words mean the same thing and one is used in 500 searches and the other in five million searches, choose the more popular term!

Once you've created your list of keywords, you'll want to use them frequently in the body of your press release to show up in as many searches as possible. Use keywords in your title, and make your title interesting, possibly a little controversial, to prompt users to need it. If you have a legitimate reason to mention a celebrity or a highly trafficked site such as Facebook or Google, do so—it will help boost search engine hits. (Avoid name-dropping if there is no logical connections; it can work against you with the search engines.)

For example, instead of writing "XYZ Company Announces New High-Tech Shampoo," try something like "Is Science the Key to Good Hair Days?" Make the science the star of the release, prominently mentioning the new shampoo as the leading example of the science in action. Clarify the user benefits without lapsing into sales language (keep it short and factual). Humor is okay if it adds to readability. Be sure that your approach, benefits, and language are all geared to your target audience.

Many press releases reach national media through press release distribution sites such as PRNewswire, PR Web, and PR Leap. Online distribution sites have rules regarding format and length. Check the rules; you may have to have different versions of your release for different sites. Many sites charge more if you go over the preferred word count. Pay attention to the rules regarding how links to Websites must be formatted within the release and how many links are permitted. Follow the rules exactly.

When given the chance, format a Web link for an e-newsletter, press release, e-book, or article as a hyperlink. The hyperlink code will make the link clickable in the online version of your release, enabling readers to click directly through to your Website.

Cut and paste your release into the body of a personalized e-mail to the specific reporter you want to reach. Send a test copy to yourself to be sure the e-mail program hasn't inserted strange-looking formatting characters or odd spacing. Reporters will not open attachments that they have not requested, so don't attach your release as a document. Avoid attaching photos or other material unless the reporter specifically asks for them. Instead, include a link where reporters can download photos, product specifications, or other materials for themselves.

Your catchy headline could appear to be spam if it's in the subject line, but you need to catch the reporter's attention. I use "Press release: (headline)" in my subject line to give reporters a heads up that the e-mail is job-related.

Make your release customer-friendly by providing a link to the exact page on your site that offers more details about the featured product/service/event and a way to purchase online. If you have a press page on your Website, include a link where reporters or customers can get more information about your company and your products. That way, motivated readers can dig deeper while you keep the release's word count to a minimum and stay focused on the main announcement.

Send your releases to each reporter individually, or use a press release distribution service. Avoid adding multiple reporters' e-mail addresses in the "to" line of your e-mail. That's unprofessional, and likely to get your release deleted. Don't add reporters to an e-mail newsletter list unless they request to hear from you regularly. Remember, you want to cultivate a good relationship with the reporters who work for the publications that reach your customers. Begin to create that relationship by being a source for useful, relevant news that makes it easier for them to do their job.

Results Reminder

Reporters are a long-term investment. Be patient and focus on how you can help them inform and entertain your common audience.

The Rule of 30

Make a list of 30 reporters who focus on areas where your news would be of value to them. Create a spreadsheet with name, publication, e-mail, phone number and specialty topic.

30

Exercises

1. Brainstorm a list of 30 topics related to your expertise that would be of interest to the reporters you have identified.

2. Think of how you can create news about those 30 topics in order to interest the reporters. Ideas include developing panel presentations, presenting teleseminars/Webinars, hosting a Meetup group, adding a case study or white paper to your Website, doing a survey and publishing the results, and so on.

Great Reasons Not to Target Mass Media (and Where You Can Focus Instead)

11

Every business owner dreams of seeing his or her press release on the front page of the *New York Times*. But did you ever stop to realize that as ego-gratifying as an above-the-fold placement in a major newspaper might be, it might completely miss your target audience?

Thirty years ago, consumers received their information differently than they do today. Back when there were only three major TV networks, all an advertiser or publicist had to do was get onto the major networks to reach most viewers. When a daily newspaper and weekly magazines were the only choice for news, the strategy was simple: get in the paper and magazines.

But times have changed. The proliferation of cable channels, satellite radio choices, online news magazines, and mobile phone applications, as well as the demise of many long-running newspapers and magazines has completely changed how consumers consume information. "Mass media" is now not nearly as "mass" as it used to be. So making the front page of a major newspaper won't help you sell products or services if your target audience doesn't read that newspaper. Welcome to a whole new world of niche marketing.

Niche Marketing Gets Results

Does the shift in consumers' media preference mean the end of mass media? No—or at least, not yet. However, that shift has dramatically reduced the effectiveness of mass media to reach the same kind of broad audience they once dominated. Believe it or not, "mass media" vehicles such as *The New York Times*, CBS, and FM radio stations have become niches themselves. Because they can't promise to reach everyone, even such long-lived media vehicles now emphasize the profile of the consumer they do reach (in other words, their niche).

Am I saying that mass media no longer plays a valuable role in promotion? No—but its role isn't what it used to be. The big newspapers, the three major broadcast networks, and big city FM radio stations can help a major advertiser saturate a market, but they reach a shrinking audience base at a very high cost per person compared with New Media alternatives. If you've got a couple of million dollars to round out your promotional campaign, go ahead and spend it with the traditional media. If you're looking for a better, more focused, and less expensive alternative, keep reading.

Refocus your idea of PR to take a broader look at the opportunities that exist for you to reach your target audience. Many people are so obsessed with having their press release picked up by a big newspaper, a major magazine, or a network TV show, that they have not bothered to study those media vehicles' audience profiles to assure that the message is reaching the right consumer. Sure, you get bragging rights if your release is picked up by a big paper, but will you get sales? It won't hurt—but how much will it help? Not only that, but what's the value of a one-shot media mention versus developing relationships with more targeted venues that provide the potential for you to reach your ideal customer over and over again?

Here's something else to consider: how often can your company generate news that is truly worthy of national attention? For most mid-sized companies, having national-caliber news might happen once or twice a year—a new product launch, an IPO, landing a huge company as a client. For solo professionals and small companies, even a once-a-year national news item might be a stretch. Publishing a new book with a major publisher would qualify, as would winning a national award or being named to a national board of directors, but beyond that, it is difficult to imagine too many opportunities that would tempt a national reporter to cover your news.

Now re-think that question, with your focus on regional/local news as well as the information sources that reach your profession or industry. Picture your ideal client and think about the blogs, Websites, podcasts, Internet radio shows, and online/offline specialty magazines, newsletters ,and member organization publications that speak directly to their interests and needs. I bet your mental wheels are turning, helping you envision all kinds of news that would be interesting and valuable to the audience most likely to buy your products or engage your services. Why not focus the majority of your effort where it is likely to make you the most sales?

Go Where Your Customers Are Already Getting Their News

If you haven't already surveyed your best customers to see what they are reading, watching, and listening to, now is the time! Online survey tools are easy to use and inexpensive. If you use Constant Contact for your e-mail newsletters, look into their survey tool to include a survey in your newsletter. Or, try out sites such as SurveyMonkey.com that provide basic survey capabilities for free.

When you target your PR to the sites and publications your best customers are already reading, you create several important advantages for your PR campaign. First, you remove the clutter of sending releases to a huge mailing list of publications that are largely not interested in your news. You can invest your time better elsewhere. Next, by shrinking the number of media outlets you're targeting, you can invest the time to get to know which reporters are covering subjects relevant to your news, so that your pitches can be perfect. Finally, and very importantly, these niche publications have already won the trust and loyalty of your best customers. They have become trusted advisors. When your news and announcements appear in these niche publications, readers are likely to accept it as a referral from a friend.

It's useful to have an idea of the nationwide size of your total target audience. Do they number in the millions (for example, small business owners or participants in multi-level marketing programs), or in the thousands (yacht owners, shipwreck enthusiasts, and so on)? Don't stop with a broad catch-all category like "small business owners." In the U.S., a company with up to 500 employees is officially a "small business." Is your target audience a "big" small business or a "small" small business?

You'll have the best results if you can get specific. For example, do you specialize in helping start-up companies, specifically those that have been in business less than three years and have sales less than $1 million? Or do you only prefer to work with companies that have been in business for more than 10 years and need to address issues with succession planning and mature markets? All "small business" is not alike. Don't be afraid to start with a fairly tight definition of your ideal customer. Once you successfully reach that narrow audience, you'll become attractive to broader audiences.

Having a fairly accurate idea of the size of your total target audience will help you target your online PR and marketing. If you know, for example, that there are 500,000 potential customers for your service, then a publication, Website or blog that reaches 50,000 people is reaching 10 percent of the total market, making it a potentially valuable outlet for your news. Without the knowledge of your total market, you might have been tempted to bypass a site that didn't have a readership in the millions (that old mass market mindset again).

You can use sites like Alexa.com to gauge traffic on the Websites, blogs, podcasts, and other online sites that you are considering for your PR outreach. Tools like Alexa.com can help you find the sites with the most traffic, meaning that getting a news item picked up by those sites is likely to put you in front of a large number of people who are ideal prospects. It can also help you gauge how many people are seeing your release on the sites where it's been posted online, and give you ideas of new sites to target with future releases that you might not have otherwise discovered.

Realize that even among sites that reach your ideal audience, size isn't the only thing that matters. Some smaller publications are read by people who are "influencers"—trend setters, authors, reporters, and others whose opinions carry a lot of weight. These sites may have a smaller audience, but the audience's importance is larger than its size. Likewise, a new site might not yet have a big following, but you might be able to establish a relationship with the blogger or site owner very easily during the online publication's early days, so that you're a trusted news source when the site gains popularity. Realize that some small sites have a very dedicated following who are true insiders within your niche audience. When your news reaches them through a site they trust, these insiders are in a position to help you grow by inviting you to speak, purchasing your product in bulk, or recommending them to their own membership. Smaller sites can be extremely influential, so don't overlook them as you build your media list.

With the continual evolution of services available via mobile phone and the advent of "smart phones" with Web and data capabilities, a growing number of consumers are reading their e-mail and surfing the Web through their phones. In the same way that permission-based e-mail marketing revolutionized promotion in the 1990s and early 2000s, mobile-phone text marketing is poised to reshape niche market promotion in the years to come.

If your message is timely and your target audience would consider it to be very important, text messaging may be a valuable tool for you. For example, restaurants and night spots can text a message to their loyal customers about dining or drink specials or nightly entertainment. Customers who make purchases on a predictable schedule might be happy to find a discount coupon in their text inbox timed for their normal purchasing habits. Sites such as MakeMeSocial.net and other providers help businesses create and manage mobile phone text campaigns. Text message marketing is here to stay, so file it away as a "maybe" for your future promotional needs.

Results Reminder

The online media sites you choose matter more for their ability to deliver your ideal audience than in their ability to deliver a huge, non-targeted audience.

The Rule of 30

Spend 30 minutes learning about the audience for your top 10 targeted sites. Review materials for online advertisers, but also read comments from readers and note the type of material that is being covered. Are you a good fit?

30

Exercises

1. Check out Alexa and similar sites such as Quantcast, StatBrain, Google Rankings, and Statsaholic to find out which of the sites targeting your ideal customer are getting the most traffic.

2. Spend at least 30 minutes exploring some of the lower-traffic sites that reach your audience and brainstorm ways they could play a role in your PR outreach through their unique voice or style.

12 The Magic of Multi-Media Releases and Online Ads

Traditional press releases were static paper documents. A big PR roll out might include pocket folders stuffed with photos, CDs or DVDs, but those extras were expensive to produce and mail in bulk, especially when reporters weren't guaranteed to use them—or even look at them.

Many businesses new to online PR and marketing make the mistake of thinking "text" when they should be thinking "interactive." Words on a screen no longer pack the same punch they did before consumers, and reporters, became accustomed to the multi-media world online. You can add more impact to your releases for very little cost by thinking sight/sound/motion when you create your PR plans.

Make It Multi-Media

In the old days, the only way to share video, audio, and photos with a press release was through a bulky, expensive press kit package. Today, all of those elements can be easily (and inexpensively) embedded into an online press release, giving the reader, and reporter, a wealth of information in an appealing sensory format.

Programs such as AudioAcrobat.com provide an affordable way to record and share Web audio without needing equipment more exotic than your phone. Whether the audio is a greeting, an interview with a CEO, or a customer testimonial, the ability to add sound to your release makes the content richer and more interesting. You can easily include the link to your Web audio recording in the body of the press release, making it easy for the reader to listen right away.

Photos also create interest and enhance your PR story. Sites such as Flickr, Shutterfly, and Google's Picasa Web all make it possible to upload digital photos from your latest event, awards program or tradeshow and share the photos through a link embedded in your press release. If you want to provide photos for reporters to publish or upload, consider having a page on your Website where you upload photos in a variety of resolutions and formats.

Web video is also an easy to add attention-getter. Small digital video cameras are widely available for less than $200. Smart phones, tablets such as the iPad, and laptop computers make it easy to create Web-ready video, edit it, and release it online. You can upload your video to YouTube or to your own Website, and then include the link in your press release, giving readers the choice to read on or view your video.

Get creative in using the multi-media options that are available to you. Consider including an audio or video testimonial from a satisfied client in your release, or a short audio clip from your president's speech. Include video from your public event, and get on-the-scene comments from attendees about how much they love the program. The trick is to keep video and audio snippets short and relevant so that they add to your release without bogging it down.

Embedded links to audio, video, and photos are especially important because most reporters won't open attachments from sources they don't know. When you have live hyperlinks in the body of your press release text, you are able to share a wealth of multi-media information without sending large attachments.

Think Beyond the Snapshot

Help readers visualize. Imagine the power of a 30-second video demonstration for your new product. Take the reader on a one-minute video tour of your new facility. Use video to give your reader a 360 degree look at your product.

Photos can provide striking before and after views that make your point more eloquently than words. If your product or service creates a visual change, you're overlooking a powerful PR tool if you're not using Web video and digital photos to augment your releases.

Realize that online PR remains accessible through search results long after your news is no longer new. If you have used good keywords to make your releases come to the top of search results, your release can continue to educate and inform reporters and prospects for weeks, months, or even years after your event is over. Your online release becomes a mini-Website to introduce a reporter or prospect to your company as well as to the news of the release itself.

If you plan to use photos or videos of event attendees or clients, be sure that you have permission. This can involve having the person sign a simple release form that allows you to use the video or audio for promotional purposes without compensation. You can also include a general release as a condition of purchasing a ticket to your event (most theme parks do this). Always be sure you show people in a flattering light in your photos and videos, and avoid any candid shots that might not look professional, such as pictures of people holding cocktails or acting silly. What was totally understandable in the moment may not look good out of context on the Web. If a photo is one where "you had to be there," don't post it!

Results Reminder

Always consider ways multi-media can punch up the impact of your online press release.

The Rule of 30

What are 30 specific examples of audio, video, and photos you can add to your upcoming news items during the course of the year?

30

Exercises

1. Create a list of the newsworthy events you can anticipate during the next 12 months. Now review your list and think about ways to add Web audio, video, and photos to increase the impact.

2. Make it a part of your standard event preparation to have a fully-charged photo-capable smart phone or tablet computer, a digital camera for still shots, and/or a digital video camera with fresh batteries, and be prepared to use them frequently!

13   Keywords Are King

Consumers and reporters often turn first to search engines such as Google for their news. When they look for information that is relevant to your products and services, how likely are they to find your Website and your press releases? Think of your own behavior as a consumer. It's rare for someone to look further than the first page of search results.

"Keywords" are the terms customers use when searching for information with a site like Google. Many companies make the mistake of focusing solely on getting their company and product name onto search engine results and forget that prospects may not yet know the name of their company or product. These valuable prospects are going to search on more generic descriptors, "used car" instead of "Ford," "plumbing services" instead of the name of a company, or "color printers" rather than a brand name product.

Use Keywords to Ensure
Your Releases Get Noticed

Start by making a list of all of the nouns you normally use to describe your company, product, service, or newsworthy event. Don't be afraid to have several variations of the same term, for example, "printer," "color printer," "laser printer," etc. Be sure that you include generic descriptions as well as brand names, product names and trademarked terms. If you've seen customers frequently misspell a term related to your product or service, include the misspelling as well.

If your product, service, or event has recently been in the news, featured in the media or associated somehow with a celebrity, include the name of the celebrity, news source or media. Do you have a well-known spokesperson or a fairly famous mascot? Include those names. Does your product, service, or event have any relevant tie-in to recent headline news stories? If so, include keywords related to that headline topic.

Now go out to Alexa and look at the most popular topics. Do any of those terms have a reasonable connection to your company, product, service, or event? If so, copy the term to your list. Sites such as Alexa may tell you what search terms are already sending business to your site and to competitors' sites. Those are definitely terms to add to your list. Go to Twitter and see what the "trending topics" are—this is a list of the most frequently tweeted terms, the terms everyone is talking about. Do any of them apply to you? If so, grab the words.

Another place to look for hot keywords is on the social bookmarking sites like Digg, Delicious, and StumbleUpon. These sites enable users to share links to articles, Websites, and other Internet content that they have found to be interesting. It's the online equivalent of hanging something on the office bulletin board with a sticky note that says "look at this." Take a few moments and look for any popular topics that are related to your news, and add the words to your list.

At this point, you should have a pretty large list. Now it's time to see which words pack the most search engine punch. Go out to Google Keyword Tool (it's free) and enter one term at a time. Google Keyword Tool will return a list of similar terms along with the number of times those terms have been used to search for a topic on Google. You'll immediately notice that many terms that are synonymous have very different frequencies of use. As I've said earlier, if you have two terms that mean the same thing and one is used a thousand times and one is used a million times, pick the million-search term!

As you're looking through the keywords generated by the program, you may get some great ideas for new words, and you may find that many of the words you started with have very low search results. Don't forget to try word combinations—sometimes a phrase does better than a single word.

When you write your press releases, use the keywords that are relevant to your topic and that get the highest search results. It's a good idea to use these top keywords in your Website copy, and in your blog as well as in your Facebook and Twitter posts. Don't be afraid to use a good keyword multiple times, but be sure that your press release is written to be attractive to human readers as well as to search engines. Avoid the temptation to mention a popular topic or celebrity just to drive up Web hits. Search engines recognize cheap tricks like that and can penalize your release in the rankings.

Remember that curiosity gets clicks, so be creative and entertaining with your press release headline. Be clever but not cute, and never mislead. Remember to use strong keywords in your headline as well as in the body of your release.

Online press-release sites often allow you to add keywords in a list. Don't skip this step! It will help your release be more visible. Your Website should have keywords and descriptive tags associated with every page as well as with photo and graphic images. Search engines can't "see" photos or graphics, so if you don't tag photos, they can't show up in search engine results. Keywords are an essential part of everything you do online.

Is It an Ad—or a Search Result?

Keywords also play a crucial role in online advertising. If you look at the first page of your Google search results, you'll notice some sites appear in a box at the top and in a column on the right. These are paid ads, and the advertisers have chosen specific keywords associated with their product or service so that when someone searches on those keywords, the ad is shown.

Google Adwords, Yahoo Search Marketing, and MSN AdCenter are just some of the keyword-driven online advertising programs available to help put your product in a prime position in front of prospects. As you may have guessed, these services aren't free, and competition can be fierce (and expensive) for popular search terms.

For example, Yahoo Search Marketing's site has a questionnaire for new prospects, and for those who are looking to create campaigns with a budget of less than $5,000/month, a pop-up box suggests they try MSN AdCenter. Need I say that before you decide to pay big bucks for a keyword tied to online advertising, it's important to test that keyword for free in your PR and on your Website to be sure it delivers a high number of click-throughs?

The trick with pay-for-keyword advertising is to identify keywords that do a great job at driving your ideal customer to your subject and that are fairly popular but that aren't the most frequently used words for that subject. Here's where you go back to the Google Keyword Tool and to your own track record using the keywords you've chosen and see if there's a "star" keyword that works for you but hasn't been discovered by everyone else. This keyword may relate to a unique feature you offer, or it may be less popular than the top words yet with a large enough search volume to satisfy your Web traffic goals.

Keywords also play an important role in Facebook ads. Facebook ads allow you to set a budget by day as well as an overall campaign cap. You can set the demographics to determine who sees your ad, and choose to pay by either impressions or click-throughs. "Impressions" refers to how many times your ad came up on other people's pages (but there's no guarantee that they read it). It's like the traffic that drives past a billboard along the highway—they may or may not be looking as they zoom by. "Click-throughs" are the number of times someone actually clicks on your ad. In the billboard analogy, it's like the people who dial the number they see on the billboard, taking action based on the promotion.

Whether you're using keywords in PR or in paid online advertising, remember that the popularity of terms (and their relevancy to your company's business) changes through time. Revisit the keywords you're using every few months to add new, more popular terms and to weed out terms that have outlived their popularity. I suggest keeping a piece of paper handy by your computer to jot down keyword ideas as you surf the Web. The Internet is constantly changing, so your campaigns need to be just as flexible and willing to adapt.

Results Reminder

Good keywords work like neon signs on the Information Highway.

The Rule of 30

Using what you now know, create a list of your top 30 keywords.

30

Exercises

1. Create a draft of your next press release using the top keywords for your topic and an attention-getting headline.

2. Even if you don't plan to do any online paid advertising right now, spend some time exploring Google Adwords, Yahoo Search Marketing, MSN AdCenter, and Facebook's ad program to learn more about the possibilities and see what choices are available within your current budget. You might be surprised!

14 Creating the Magic Media List for Your Topic

As you've read through the book, I've asked you to make some preliminary lists of bloggers, reporters, and other members of traditional and online media who might be good prospects for your news and press releases. In this chapter, we'll refine those lists into a power tool that will become the backbone of your online PR and marketing outreach.

Refining Your Roster of Reporters

Pull out the draft you've been working on of reporters and key contacts. I would suggest building your media list in a spreadsheet program such as Microsoft Excel to make it easy to view and update. Here are the key elements your media list should include:

- ~ Reporter/blogger/host name.
- ~ Contact e-mail (best if it is directly to the reporter/host and not a general "info" e-mail).
- ~ Phone number for follow up calls.

~ Website.

~ Notes to help you target the right news to the right person.

It is absolutely essential that you have a name for the reporter/blogger/host you want to reach. Nothing turns off a reporter more than to get an e-mail addressed to "Dear Sir or Madam" or "Dear Editor." (By the way, unless it is the only contact person named and it's a very small publication, don't send your news to the publication's editor. Find the individual reporter/blogger who handles that topic.) Remember that successful PR isn't about blasting out releases to the largest list possible; instead, it's about cultivating win-win relationships with gatekeepers and consumers who share your information because it is valuable to their audiences.

Without a contact e-mail, you won't be able to send your press release. I'm not a big fan of e-mail forms on Websites. I much prefer a real e-mail address. However, if your only choice is a contact form and the site is a good match for your topic, send a preliminary e-mail explaining your need and ask to whom you should send your information. Assuming someone is minding the store, you should get a response directing you to some other e-mail used for press releases.

Phone numbers should be used sparingly. I've had many professional reporters and radio/TV hosts tell me that it takes a minimum of seven contacts to get a reporter's attention. The majority of these contacts should come via e-mail to be less intrusive. However, if you have sent your release and followed up several times via e-mail, and it is an important newsworthy item (not just important to you, but to the target audience), then it's okay to make a brief follow-up call. Give your name and company name, and no more than a one-sentence recap of the release, mentioning that you had e-mailed it and wanted to be sure it was received. Offer to re-send it if they did not receive it, and leave your name, phone number, and e-mail address. Don't beg or threaten or go into sales mode. If your news appeals to them, they're likely to call. If not, just assume that it wasn't a good fit this time, and try again on the next release.

Visit the Website to be sure that your topic hasn't been recently featured, and to get a feel for the style and tone. Review what the site covers and the slant it takes to confirm that it is a good fit for your audience and this particular release. You don't have to send every release to everyone on your media list. Build a reputation for being a good news source by only sending releases to the people most interested in the topic, and avoid cluttering up the inbox of reporters who won't be interested (they'll remember, and not in a good way).

In the notes section, jot information to help the next round of releases be more successful. For example, find out how often the site/blog updates with new material. If you missed the deadline this time, make a note of it for next time. If you have a conversation with a reporter/blogger via e-mail or phone, write down what you learned about upcoming topics being researched and things they don't cover at all. This will help you send the right material next time, which builds trust and credibility.

If the site has information that documents their target reader or listener, review it, but don't believe everything you read. Unless the information is formally audited, there's no way to know for sure. However, the way the site describes its audience should make sense given what you see on the site itself. Don't base your choices on age and income alone. Be on the lookout for sites that really focus on your niche.

For really big news, send the release to a national audience. Compiling the list yourself is a large and time-consuming task. Media people change jobs frequently, so your list may be outdated by the next time you need it. I suggest paying the money to send out a national release via sites like PR Newswire or PRWeb. These sites are in business to send out releases successfully, and they have the manpower to keep their lists updated.

Remember that online PR must meet the needs of the consumer as well as the reporter. Make the news valuable enough to both move the reader to action and encourage the reader to share the information with his or her network of friends and followers. Focus on user benefit (without going into sales language) rather than listing features. If you have a special discount, promotion, or bonus, be sure to mention it. Provide a link to the product page (which should have a "buy now" link) and not just to your home page. Make it easy for a consumer to consume your product!

Set Your Sights on Multi-Media Publicity

In today's online PR and marketing world, your opportunities for promotion go far beyond newspapers, magazines, TV, and radio. Some people believe that online media is somehow inferior to traditional media. Nothing could be further from the truth! In fact, online media is gradually supplanting many traditional forms of media, such as printed newspapers, due to cost constraints and changes in consumer taste and consumption patterns. Ignore online media at your peril—it's definitely the wave of the future.

Most newspapers and magazines now have some form of online presence. Some permit the general public to read all or most of their contents, while others offer expanded and premium content for subscribers only. Realize that free content reaches a much broader audience than the publication's subscription base. That's really good for you, and for your press release, because you gain two important advantages: a larger readership and an online mention that boosts your search engine presence.

As publications move online (or new online-only publications are created), they are no longer limited by the costs of traditional printing. Adding one or 100 new pages online has a negligible cost. The 24/7 nature of the Internet news cycle also puts editors under pressure to constantly update their sites or "lose eyeballs" to sites with fresher news. That means that newspapers and magazines must add additional online content beyond what fit in the physical publication in order to compete. Editors need more news content, more articles, more lifestyle features, more events, and more content— helpfully supplied in large part by press releases and article pitches from companies like yours. The additional benefit of online content is the ability to include a video or audio snippet, or to share color photos of an event or product. Consumers like multi-media, and so do editors. If you can supply video, audio, and digital photos, be sure to mention this at the bottom of the release (either embed links or add a line that says "photos, video, and audio available upon request").

Online newsletters are also fertile ground for press releases and article suggestions. All kinds of business newsletters are posted online, uploaded to Facebook, and linked to Twitter in addition to being sent out to permission-based lists of thousands of readers. The editors of these newsletters are constantly looking for news, interviews, products, or books to review; opinion pieces; and industry information, as well as quips and quotes.

Where do you find these newsletters? Everywhere. Your clients, vendors, and suppliers create some of these newsletters, and they also can recommend good ones produced by other businesses. Trade and professional associations have online newsletters, as do Chambers of Commerce, membership organizations, and industry thought leaders. Few of these newsletter producers can create as much content as they need by themselves. Today's online newsletters can also feature Web audio and video as well as digital photos. Newsletter editors are open to good sources, but are wary of being deluged by press releases that don't hit the mark.

Blogs are another often-overlooked opportunity for news. Bloggers, like newsletter editors, are often business people who are sharing insights on topics related to their area of expertise. They blog to discuss ideas, not for the purpose of reporting news or promoting other people's products. But if you approach them in the right way, they may find your information to be in line with their purpose, and feature you, your comments, or your services. Blogs also feature Web audio and video and digital photos, but the material must be compelling for its content and not heavily promotional.

What's the trick to approaching online newsletter editors and bloggers? Respect. These gatekeepers don't see themselves as traditional reporters, and they usually don't have a formal journalism background. They are driven by a need to share helpful information, and they're often very protective of their readers. The key to winning over newsletter editors and bloggers is to create a relationship first, then ask if there's a need to supply content. You can begin that relationship by sending an e-mail about a post or issue that you particularly liked, or by becoming a regular, positive commenter to posts and issues online. Include your real name, company and e-mail address in all of your comments. Write comments that support and amplify what the editor or blogger has written, and make your input thoughtful and meaningful. If you have the opportunity to meet the editor or blogger at an event, make it a point to introduce yourself.

Ease your way into offering highly targeted, infrequent, and on-the-mark news or guest posts. If you get a "yes," don't abuse the privilege—it's not an invitation to spam them with everything you've got. Carefully nurtured, these vehicles can be a very powerful and credible way to spread your news online.

Broadcast and satellite radio aren't your only options to be a featured guest. Internet radio sites have sprung up all over the Web and some established shows reach tens of thousands (or millions) of dedicated listeners. Sites like BlogTalkRadio, TalkZone, LATalkRadio, and VoiceAmerica all feature talk radio shows that are delivered via the Internet. Because these shows have none of the overhead of broadcast radio, they can focus on highly specific topics, niche audiences, and targeted interests that deliver a valuable focused audience. Don't worry too much about the size of their listenership—if the show delivers your ideal target audience, even a few hundred dedicated listeners might produce a nice spike in sales in exchange for a few minutes of your time. Consider subscribing to RadioGuestList. com's regular e-mails highlighting which Internet radio shows are looking for guests.

Podcasts are very similar to Internet radio. Listeners can visit the podcast site to hear the show online, download to an MP3 player, or subscribe so that they never miss a future show. Most podcasts are also distributed (often for free) via iTunes, making them available to a broad audience. The majority of Internet radio shows also offer a podcast for listeners who did not catch the show live.

Podcasts and Internet radio shows often have a page that describes how to contact the host and pitch yourself as a guest. Make sure to read and follow these guidelines if you want to be considered. Think carefully about your suggested topic, to make sure it fits the audience and has the ability to inform and entertain. Position yourself as an expert, and include a (very short) bio to support your credibility. For a great e-book on how to pitch yourself to radio hosts, I recommend Wayne Kelly's OnAirPublicity.com.

Online publicity opportunities abound, but they require the same respect and professional approach you would accord to traditional media. Because the Internet never sleeps, online media creators have an insatiable need for news, information, interviews, product/book news, and multi-media, but it must meet the needs of their very targeted audiences. Take the time to approach these outlets right and your news could rocket to the top of the search engine results.

Results Reminder

Look for ways your news can feed the Internet's insatiable need for content.

The Rule of 30

What are 30 newsworthy topics that relate to your expertise?

30

Exercises

1. Start paying attention to the e-mail newsletters that you receive, and ask your colleagues and clients for their recommendations. Add the newsletters that are a good fit for your focus to your media spreadsheet.

2. Spend 30 minutes browsing through shows on BlogTalkRadio. com and similar platforms. Make a note of the shows best suited to your topic.

15 Your Online Press Kit

A press kit is the combination of information that public relations professionals put together to send out to reporters, TV hosts, and local radio in advance of a major news announcement or big event. In the old days, these kits filled a shallow mailing box or a stuffed-to-bursting pocket folder, and included photos, CDs, DVDs, press releases, background material, and other information intended to help news organizations cover an event thoroughly and accurately. The kits were expensive to create, and there was a high degree of waste, because many reporters ended up trashing the information if it didn't fit their space or deadlines.

Fast-forward to the Age of the Internet. Though a few very large companies still sometimes engage PR firms to send out traditional press kits for a major announcement, most have recognized the benefit to moving their press kits online. The greatest thing about the online press kit is that costs plummet while reach grows far beyond what any company could afford as a mailing.

Press kits are like business cards; if you don't have one, you have no way to make an introduction and no way to provide valuable information to people with whom you want to do business. By putting the power of your press kit to work for you, your company can enjoy more accurate media coverage, more exposure for story ideas, and more complete information through press coverage.

You can create a very effective and robust online press kit that provides value to reporters and consumers alike—and helps you build visibility.

The Basics of Your Press Kit

A press kit's most important purpose is to help reporters who want to write about your company, product, services, book, or event do so with complete and accurate information. Set aside a page on your Website and make it easy to find off your main navigation with a title like "News and Events."

Some of the key elements of a press kit include executive bios, a company history, fact sheets, backgrounders, testimonials, recent speeches, recent major press releases, and information regarding recent recalls or high-profile crises (and how they are being dealt with).

Reviews, awards, story ideas, Web audio and video clips, and virtual tours can make for an interesting and interactive press kit. Posting a press kit is a reason in itself for sending out a release and inviting the press to take a look. You can add a link to your press kit in your e-mail signature when you pitch reporters, bloggers, and radio/TV hosts, giving them an instant way to get more information.

Let's discuss each of the pieces that normally go into a basic press kit, and then talk a little bit about the extras you can add to really make the most of a Web-based kit.

~ Executive bios. For most small businesses, this means the bios of the owner and possibly the founder. A bio is not a resume. Your bio should include a current professional head-shot photo and a few key highlights from your experience that underscore your credibility and expertise. Keep it short, and focus on what customers most need to know.

~ Company history. Give a short (three or four paragraphs at the most) recap of your company's major milestones, including the date founded, major expansions or product launch dates, significant awards, and other key news. End on an upbeat note with mention of your most important recent news.

~ Fact sheets. A fact sheet is a very short and to-the-point recap of the items a reporter most needs to know to cover your company accurately. This includes the president's name, the date and location the company was founded, main product names, number of employees, and other key information. Fact sheets are very brief, intended to be easily scanned by a reporter who wants to double check a date, name, or number. They usually take a format like this: "Date founded: 1984." Have the description of the data left-justified, and align the brief responses in a right-hand column. Fact-sheet information should be single words, short phrases, or fragment sentences—keep it short!

~ Backgrounders. A backgrounder helps a reporter (or potential customer) learn more about the history of an event or product. For example, a company that has hosted a golf tournament for 20 years might include a backgrounder with headings like "The History of the Harding Invitational Open," "Past Harding Invitational Winners," "Celebrities Who Have Played at the Harding Invitational Open," "The Harding Invitational Prize Purse," and so on. Limit the information to one or two pages at the most, and each item to only a short paragraph. In backgrounders, it's okay to use full sentences, but keep them short and sweet.

~ Press releases. Your online News page is a great place to post all of your most recent press releases. Not only does it enable a reporter or prospect to find your news at a glance, but it also increases the search engine hits mentioning your company and products.

~ Testimonials and speeches. Use the power of Web audio to share short audio clips from recent speeches and testimonials from clients. Accompany the audio clip with digital photographs for even more punch.

~ Recalls and crises. It's essential for you to take the lead in providing information, or you cede control to others to position your company. If your company has recalled a product, your News page should provide information on how affected consumers can return damaged products and get a refund. When a crisis strikes, use your News page to let reporters and other stakeholders know how your company is dealing with the situation and what measures are being put in place to keep the problem from happening again.

~ Extras. Your online press kit can make it very easy for reporters, bloggers and TV/radio hosts to feature you and your company. Consider posting digital photos of your headshot and major products in various sizes and resolutions so that a blogger who wants to put your photo with your guest post doesn't have to track someone down to e-mail the picture. Create short (less than five minutes) clips from the videos of recent Webinars or speeches presented by your company. Use Web video for short product demonstrations. Utilize 360-degree photography to show your products to their best advantage. Provide downloadable product specification pages. Don't waste a great opportunity for reporters or customers who want to dig further!

Using Your Press Kit

I've already mentioned one great way to use your press kit/News page—include a link as part of your e-mail signature. This is a must-have when you send out press releases, but it's not a bad thing to have as a regular part of your signature for every e-mail you send. What a great way to encourage prospects and contacts to learn more about your company!

Once the basic pieces are in place, press kits can be customized for special events, corporate anniversaries, new product launches, and other major occasions. Add a new fact sheet about the occasion, include fresh audio and video clips, tuck in some pertinent quotes by executives on the occasion, and perhaps include a whole or partial speech text if appropriate.

If you create good-quality online press kit materials, you can also easily print them out when a situation, such as a client meeting, would benefit from an information piece to leave behind. Share your online press kit through a hyperlink as a follow-up with event and trade show attendees at a fraction of the cost of mailing printed materials.

Online press kits make it easy to create lively documents, such as interactive timelines and milestones complete with audio and video. If you've created TV or YouTube commercials, post them on your News page as well. Don't forget to feature links to your company blog, podcast, or YouTube channel. Make it easy for readers to find your Twitter, Facebook, and other social media pages. Many companies upload their press releases on a blog that is embedded onto the Webpage, making it possible for reporters who frequently cover their company or industry to subscribe and receive new releases automatically via RSS (a simple subscription tool that is part of most blogs).

Be sure to update your News page frequently. Don't just use press releases to tell consumers and the media that an event is going to happen—provide your own coverage of what went on, complete with photos and a recap that reporters, bloggers, and newsletter editors are welcome to reuse to cover your event. Add Web video and digital photos of your events, trade shows, and product launches, including man-in-the-street audio clips from customers and participants. By featuring your own coverage of your newsworthy events, you increase the ability for the information to be found in search engine results, and you increase the likelihood that a reporter who is pressed for time may utilize your information—possibly verbatim—to provide a recap.

Online press kits offer an exciting range of opportunities for you to tell your story in an interactive, compelling way to both consumers and the media. Use your imagination to take full advantage of all the Internet has to offer.

Results Reminder

Your press kit is like an expanded business card—take full advantage of it!

The Rule of 30

What are 30 items you could include in your online press kit?

30

Exercise

Spend 30 minutes determining which of the items for your online press kit already exist in digital form and which will need to be scanned or converted.

16 Distributing Your Release Online

A press release is an announcement designed to be sent out to reporters in hopes of gaining media placement and attention. Today's press release works even harder, because with the Internet, your announcement can reach consumers, as well as gatekeepers such as bloggers, e-newsletter editors, Website owners, and Twitter mavens.

Your online releases also increase your company's search engine hits, and the inbound link to your Website from the release increases your site's "relevancy" for search engines and directories. Another plus is the long-lasting marketing impact your releases can make through time. Once posted, your release lasts forever in cyberspace.

Local, regional, and national reporters rely on online news release sites to help them fill the never-ending demand for content created by a 24/7 news cycle. You need to be represented.

Free Versus Paid Online Distribution

The first decision you will need to make is the choice between free and paid press-release distribution. Of course, you'll be sending the press release out to your local reporter and blogger contacts (embedded in the body of the e-mail, not as an attachment), so that level of distribution is automatically free. But once you go beyond your own list, you're confronted with choices on how best to reach the next tier of industry publications and national/regional reporters.

PRNewswire.com and similar paid sites usually offer editing services, highly segmented mailing lists, a large national distribution roster, an attractive site displaying recent releases, and sophisticated tracking to help you see how effectively your release has reached its audience. The cost of sending out a release through a paid site varies depending on the lists chosen, the length of the release and the extra services added.

Releases sent through paid sites go through a review process to cut down on spam and pornography. The sites pose their own list of rules, word counts, and caveats, and these are strictly followed. Many of the paid sites offer the option to have your release written or edited (for an extra fee), and may provide a phone consultant to help you choose the right level of distribution. Paid sites also often offer extras such as video links, Tweets about your release, search engine optimization, and enhanced tracking.

Free sites, such as PRLog.com, offer fewer extras (such as editing), and may not offer as large or as highly segmented mailing lists. Free sites vary in attractiveness. Most provide some required review to avoid spam and inappropriate content, but some operate on a buyer-beware approach. Extra services, such as editing or writing, are less common. On the other hand, distribution through these sites is truly free, making your release widely accessible. Many sites offer at least a basic level of tracking to let you see how often your release was viewed and the number of impressions it made.

How do you know whether your release should be sent through a paid or a free distribution site? I work with both types of sites, and I consider them to be tools for different kinds of jobs, much like the difference between owning a regular screwdriver and a power screwdriver. The key to success is knowing which job requires which tool.

If you have major news of national importance, consider a paid press release. Realize that "national importance" is true for only a small subset of all releases sent. Most small companies and solo professionals may have nationally important announcements only once every year or so.

What constitutes "national importance"? To me, a release is nationally important if it affects a product or service available nationwide (or globally), if it affects financial markets or the lives of people all over the country, or if it represents a certified milestone, such as the first (or millionth) of its kind.

Here are some types of news that is nationally important:

~ Book releases.
~ New product releases.
~ Mergers and acquisitions.
~ Initial Product Offerings (IPOs).
~ Quarterly reports of publically traded companies (distribution is defined and required by law).
~ Major awards and certified record-breaking milestones.
~ Appointment to leadership in a national company or a national association.
~ Opening new locations outside of a single geographic area or the announcement of a firm opening up to franchising or licensing.
~ Events or contests open for national participation.
~ Signing a deal with a major celebrity or corporate partner.
~ Quirky, one-of-a-kind feature news, such as serving the millionth customer, cooking the world's biggest pancake, or the 50th birthday of the world's largest pink stucco cow statue.

If your news doesn't fit one of those categories, you have two options. You might use a less-expensive paid release distribution site, or you could consider free distribution. I use free distribution to augment paid distribution, because this is a situation where more is better. When a client has a release that isn't nationally important, the least expensive paid distribution in combination with free distribution works well to make the release highly visible online for a low cost.

Many companies send out multiple releases each month, and can't afford paid distribution for all of them. Budget is certainly a strong reason to use free distribution, especially for less important releases. I advise clients to use the more expensive distribution for one or two essential releases and fall back to the free or less costly distribution alternatives for their "routine" announcements.

The biggest downside to free sites is that it's possible to get lost in the noise on their "new releases" page due to the sheer volume of releases posted. Because the sites are free, no release will stay at the top of the page for long as newer releases are added every minute. In addition, the free sites don't enjoy the same brand recognition of older, established paid sites such as PRNewswire, and some reporters may check sites they're more familiar with more often.

At the same time, realize that good keywords will make or break your release whether it is paid or free distribution. Paying for distribution doesn't relieve you of the need to choose keywords carefully and craft a strong headline. Search engines don't know or care whether you paid for distribution; content is king.

Here are some types of releases that work best as free distribution:

- ~ News of local or regional interest.
- ~ Routine promotions and hirings.
- ~ Local events and routine public meetings.
- ~ Participation in local leadership positions.
- ~ Roster of speakers or guests for regional, online or local events and radio/TV shows or upcoming blog guests.
- ~ New products or locations that are not national in scale.

Free distribution of your release can still reach the same reporters, consumers, and decision makers who read the paid releases. That's because your free release will still be searchable and will show up on search engine results pages. If you're careful to use powerful keywords throughout the release and craft a good headline, even a free distribution release can attract national attention.

Free distribution works very well for monthly releases, such as upcoming speakers for a club or routine meeting. These events would not merit either the price or the services of one of the paid distribution sites, but there is a compelling reason to have the information searchable online. Whether you use free or paid releases, be sure that your release is well written, free of typos and grammatical errors, and designed to be keyword-searchable.

A Closer Look at Some Top Paid and Free Distribution Sites

Distribution sites change their prices and services frequently, so I'll avoid mentioning site-specific details that could change, but let's look at some of the major features offered by a few of the most popular paid and free distribution sites.

A Quick Tour of What Paid Sites Offer

PRNewswire is the granddaddy of press release distribution, with a history that has spanned regular postal mail, fax, and now e-mail. Two other popular paid sites are PRWeb and PRLeap, offering release distribution at a variety of price points with a spectrum of extra options and services (for an additional price).

Some of the services offered by these and other paid distribution sites include:

~ The ability to distribute a release via fax and/or e-mail.

~ Highly targeted and segmented mailing lists, including trade shows, industry-specific journals and magazines, and a large variety of interest categories for regional and national packages.

~ International distribution with regional and industry sub-lists and the ability to reach individual reporters as well as translation services.

~ Integration with social media beyond a simple Facebook link, including services to utilize social bookmarking, target niche bloggers, and make it easy for readers to share the release with others.

~ Sophisticated search engine optimization.

~ More options for including photos and video with releases, including the ability to have photos displayed on large LED display boards in major cities.

~ Special packages designed expressly for the needs of investor relations and non-profit PR.

~ Ongoing efforts to woo journalists via online newsrooms.

~ Specialized Web hosting, storage for online data, and the creation and hosting of branded online newsrooms for individual clients.

~ Extended tracking and monitoring capabilities for detailed metrics.

~ Online forms to make it easy to build a release and find good keywords.

~ Distribution to the major news outlets: AP, UPI, Reuters, and so on.

Of course, nothing on the list is free at these sites. Pricing often includes strict word counts, and going over the word count can result in hefty extra fees. Few sites offer help with writing and editing, and those services also come with additional fees. There are no guarantees of placement in any major newspaper or Website. That's why it's so important to determine whether or not your release is of national importance before you select a distribution site. You can pay hundreds of dollars to send a release about your local ice cream social fundraiser to the AP Wire, but no one at CNN is going to care.

A Look at What Free Sites Have to Offer

For comparison, check out free distribution sites like PRLog.com, Free-Press-Release.com, and PR.com. These sites offer a mix of free and low-cost paid distribution, and a more scaled-down, basic set of services. In general, you can expect to find the following on free distribution sites:

~ Fewer options for search engine optimization and social media integration.

~ Distribution focused to online sites and search engines but not the major newswires or print publications.

~ Distribution by category or region, but no ability to choose a list targeted to reporters by name.

~ Fewer categories and less targeted reach for industry-specific news.

~ More limited word count, fewer video and photo links, limited ability to include active Web addresses or hyperlinks.

~ Limited tracking and metrics.

~ The ability offered by some to place articles and job postings as well as press releases, and possibly the inclusion of your company in an online business directory.

~ Free distribution to major search engines and keyword searchability.

Because free distribution sites don't charge for releases, they pay for their costs by selling advertising. This means that the page showcasing all the newest releases will have paid banner or block ads for other companies and services.

Sure, these sites have limitations, but did I mention that they're free? F-R-E-E. They may not have a pretty home page or as many options available, but they provide a valuable service just by getting your release out on the Internet and distributed to their partner sites. In conjunction with your paid release or as a stand-alone for more minor or routine news announcements, these sites help to boost your search engine results and put your release in front of consumers as well as the news media. They provide a valuable service when used correctly.

Blogs and Your News Release

As a general rule, bloggers don't like to be deluged with press releases. On the other hand, bloggers still need a continual source for fresh content and offbeat stories. The difference is in the approach.

Never send a press release to a blogger without permission. Start by finding a contact for the blog via e-mail or Facebook, and make a personal connection. Study the blog to be sure your information is a good fit by subject and audience. Ask the blogger what kinds of stories or topics they're looking for, and offer to help if your news fits. Let the blogger know what news, commentary, or information you can provide, and ask what format they prefer. At that point, some may invite you to send it in release form. Others may ask for an article or blog post, or prefer a link to your site to gather the news yourself. Give them what they want in the format they prefer, and don't take a single "yes" as permission to send everything. Be choosy about how often you contact a blogger and be sure that you only send correctly targeted information.

Your own blog should be a partner in your PR efforts. Though I'd avoid running your release in press release format, consider re-writing it to read like an article or blog post. On your own blog, you can provide frequent updates on an event, discuss the impact post-event, or chronicle a product launch or new location opening. Be sure to use keywords in your blog entries, and utilize the blog's capabilities to add tags and categories for maximum searchability. You can also tweet about your news on Twitter, add updates on your Facebook and LinkedIn pages, and include the information in your e-newsletter. Utilize every resource to spread the word.

Results Reminder

Use the right tool for the right reason to get the best results at the lowest cost.

The Rule of 30

Spend 30 minutes getting to know your options for free and paid press release distribution by visiting the top sites.

30

Exercises

1. Look at your list of annual and upcoming newsworthy events. Divide them into two categories: "national" news and major announcements vs. local news and routine updates.

2. Now that you're familiar with the free and paid distribution sites, review the different levels of services offered by the paid sites and their range of paid services. Match the price/services options to each of your releases that are candidates for paid distribution. (Don't fall into the trap of paying top dollar for every release. Buy only the services you need.)

The Multiplyer Magic of Autoresponder Marketing

17

Often when we think of "online marketing" and "online PR," we think of the glitzy tools such as press release distribution sites, banner ads, and search engine optimization. But the lowly autoresponder is a powerful and yet often overlooked tool in your online marketing and PR arsenal.

An "autoresponder" is a pre-programmed series of e-mail messages that are triggered by a customer's action. For example, someone who opts in to your list by signing up for a free article might trigger a series of three or four e-mails about other products, special discounts, or upcoming events. Someone who has purchased a product might get an autoresponder message offering extra savings for an immediate additional purchase, or to simply say "thank you."

Autoresponder Basics

Autoresponders vary according to the program, but they have several features in common. Here are some of the most common:

~ Ability to program one or more follow-up e-mails triggered by a specific event.

~ Ability to program different content for autoresponder e-mails determined by different trigger events.

~ Ability to set an interval between follow-up e-mails, anywhere from a few hours to several days (some programs allow follow-ups for a full year).

Autoresponders, when used creatively, can help you sell additional products/services, educate buyers about upcoming events or other offerings, and deepen your customer relationship. One popular use of autoresponders is to provide a free series of e-mail "classes" on a topic featuring articles, video links, and audio clips. You are limited only by your imagination and the constraints of your autoresponder program.

Developing Loyalty and Overcoming Resistance With Autoresponders

Consider using an autoresponder to draw a prospect further down your sales funnel. A "sales funnel" is the array of products and services you offer, starting with those that are free or least expensive and progressing to your priciest offerings. Use an autoresponder to connect with someone who has requested a free white paper or article, and draw them down your funnel by suggesting other entry-priced products or services they might need. Or, use an autoresponder to thank a purchaser of one of your products and offer additional bonus items or gifts to increase loyalty and satisfaction.

Autoresponders can be very important in overcoming buyer remorse and creating post-purchase satisfaction. "Buyer remorse" is the feeling of regret that sets in after making a large purchase. Many people second-guess themselves, wondering if they should have spent the money or might have gotten a better deal elsewhere. Depending on the purchase, this can lead to cancelled contracts or returned products. The buyer has lost sight of the value he or she initially saw in the product and now is focused solely on price.

Now imagine that an hour after making the purchase, the buyer receives an e-mail thanking him for the sale and reinforcing the value, including a few testimonials from other happy customers. The next day, another e-mail arrives, checking in to see how he likes the product, reminding him of the availability of customer support to answer any questions, and suggesting some ways to get additional use or value from the purchase. A few days later, another e-mail lets him know about a free training teleseminar, or provides a link to an online tutorial or other resource to extend the usefulness of the product. If there's a user community, the new purchaser can be invited to join via autoresponder, and can be provided with the links to your company's social media sites to be part of the conversation.

Using autoresponders in this manner creates "post-purchase satisfaction," which is the feeling of validation that a good choice has been made. It's the opposite of buyer's remorse. Customers want to be reassured that they have made a good choice, gotten a great value, and spent money wisely. The more expensive the purchase, the more urgent the need for validation.

Even a relatively inexpensive purchase can be the trigger for an autoresponder sequence that encourages additional sales or frequent participation. For example, someone who buys a book might receive autoresponders offering related teleclasses, coaching programs, and DVDs. A customer who buys a piece of equipment might be glad to know about optional extras and add-ons or training programs. When presented as service supporting a sale and done without a heavy sales push, these messages are viewed as helpful instead of intrusive, and encourage a customer to feel supported and treated well.

Another benefit of autoresponders is their ability to provide a digital "free sample." When a prospect signs up for a newsletter or makes a purchase, an autoresponder can provide a downloadable free sample of another product or service. For example, a customer who buys one book might receive an autoresponder e-mail with a link to a free chapter from another related book, and a trial subscription to an add-on product/service. A prospect who has requested a free article or e-book might receive an autoresponder e-mail with a mini e-course, with three to five sequential e-mails offering tips and insights. When you remember that autoresponders can include links to Web pages, video and audio, they become very powerful ways to provide value and add a personal touch.

Autoresponders are the automated version of "Do you want fries with that?" They're an online marketing tool for suggestive selling, and they can provide a great way to provide enhanced customer service and increase perceived satisfaction.

Results Reminder

Autoresponders add an important personal touch to remind buyers of the full value of their purchase.

The Rule of 30

Remember your 30 Magic Touches? Autoresponders can provide several of those touches to help prospects become customers.

30

Exercises

1. Look at the products you are offering for sale via online purchase. How could you use autoresponders to overcome buyer's remorse and increase post-purchase satisfaction?

2. Now think about the items you offer to entice prospects to opt into your mailing list. What autoresponder messages might enhance the value and draw them further into your sales funnel?

Rule the "Airwaves" With Internet Radio and Podcasts, Virtual Video, and Web TV

18

Once upon a time, not very long ago, the only radio stations you could listen to were the ones whose signal carried over the airwaves to where you lived. Back in the day, if you wanted to reach listeners whose radios wouldn't pick up your local radio station's signal, your only choice was to buy airtime on their local radio station. Mega stations with a broader reach were few, far between, and expensive.

Satellite radio and Internet radio changed all that. Today's listeners expect to hear their favorite shows via the Internet, and via satellite, no matter where they travel. If you don't like the hosts or shows in your local market, you can hear stations from anywhere, and grab the programs you like live or recorded.

Internet radio is part of the online marketing and PR world you need to get to know. "Internet radio" means radio that you listen to via your computer and an Internet connection, as opposed to via the airwaves. In this sense, the term "radio" is a bit of a misnomer, because many "Internet radio" programs do not originate with a real FCC-licensed radio station, nor do they utilize radio technology to reach you through your computer. The term sticks because it's convenient. "Internet TV" carries the same disclaimer, and "podcast" refers to a recorded and downloadable audio, but it doesn't require that you listen with an iPod.

A "Brave New World" for Broadcasting

Internet radio began when audio could be successfully sent without crashing the listener's computer due to huge file sizes. Once the technological barrier was removed, lots of passionate pioneers jumped in to create audio shows for every interest and taste. Traditional radio stations caught on a little later, realizing that they could expand their listener base by broadcasting over the Internet as well as via the airwaves.

As of the writing of this book, Internet radio isn't limited by the same FCC rules as broadcast radio, making the barriers to entry very low. Anyone with a phone, a headset, and a computer can create a radio show and share it with millions of people. This democratization means that you'll find shows on absolutely every topic and hosts ranging from polished professionals to rank amateurs.

The real beauty of Internet radio lies in its segmentation. Traditional radio stations were limited in their programming because they had to find sponsors to underwrite their shows. It's expensive to run a traditional radio station, given the staff, FCC license fees, equipment, and so on. Eclectic tastes in topics often went underserved, were relegated to lower quality AM stations, or showed up with middle-of-the-night program slots.

Because Internet radio has almost no overhead costs, shows can run on the passion of their creators. This means that any and every topic can find a home—and very possibly, a world-wide niche audience of fans.

Everything I've said about Internet radio is also true of Internet TV. The video technology has lagged a little behind the audio technology, but it's caught up quickly. Not only are regular network shows turning up on sites such as Hulu.com, but direct-to-Internet original programming now rules YouTube, Vimeo, and other on-demand sites. Some of this Internet video looks like home movies, and some is fully professional. Performers and bands have discovered that uploading music videos to YouTube and similar sites has a positive effect on sales. These sites have helped previously unknown singers launch successful careers.

Podcasts are really a subset of Internet radio. Podcasts provide a downloadable audio file that can be listened to on an MP3 player (such as an iPod) as well as on a computer. Many Internet radio shows that broadcast live also provide podcast recordings for people who missed the show. A lot of programming is created especially for podcast listeners, who subscribe and receive automatic downloads of the newest recordings.

You can find plenty of Internet radio shows on sites such as BlogTalkRadio and DivaToolbox. Look for Podcasts on sites such as PodcastPickle and PodcastAlley. One free service, RadioGuestList. com, lets you know about Internet radio shows that are looking for guests and provides contact information.

Internet radio, TV, and podcasting offer two types of value for business owners: they create a large new opportunity for PR via interviews, and they present a highly focused niche market for online advertising.

The Three Flavors of Internet Radio

When it comes to using Internet radio for publicity purposes, there are three basic flavors of shows: pay-for-play, free to guests, and paid advertising.

Pay-for-Play

Some Internet radio shows (especially those that boast about being part of major traditional radio and/or satellite networks) are set up when a host purchases a block of airtime from another, larger organization. The host then seeks to recoup costs by asking guests to pay for the privilege of being interviewed. Some of these shows have been in existence for a long time and have built a large and dedicated audience. Others have "celebrity" hosts who are well-connected enough to have famous-name guests. The famous-name guests often don't pay for their interview because they draw listeners and attract less well-known guests (who do pay for airtime).

Fees for pay-for-play interviews can range widely, from hundreds to thousands of dollars. Before you decide to pay for an Internet radio interview, be sure you do your homework to assure that you're getting value for your money. Ask to see audited reports on listenership. Verify their download numbers. See how well the site turns up in search engine results, and dig deep to ensure that the site delivers a large enough slice of your ideal target audience to be worth the price.

Remember, there are plenty of traditional and Internet radio shows that do not charge guests for interviews, so think twice before paying for what is essentially an infomercial. Just because a show asks you to pay does not mean that the show offers a larger or better targeted audience than similar "free" shows.

Free to Guests

Traditional broadcast radio (or TV) does not charge a fee for guests to be interviewed. It's up to the host or program director to find and book guests of interest to the show's audience, which provides value to both the show and to the guest.

A great many Internet radio shows also do not charge guests to be interviewed. These shows may subsidize their programming with paid advertising (as do broadcast radio shows), or (given the low overhead of Internet radio) may do the show out of pure passion for the topic. Often, the shows that have lively and loyal listenerships are those that are moderated by a host with a true passion for the subject.

Internet radio makes it possible to provide programming even for fairly small niche audiences because the audience size doesn't have to attract major advertisers. A small, very active following for a show might be perfect for your PR and online marketing goals if it delivers your ideal target audience. Remember that radio hosts become trusted friends to their listeners, who consider exposure to the show's guests a type of personal introduction. Exposure on these kinds of shows can be very valuable for gaining visibility and credibility among key target audiences.

Never consider an interview on an Internet radio show to be "second class" compared to a traditional broadcast interview. Many Internet radio hosts have a broadcast media background, and conduct equally polished interviews with a professional level of post-production editing. These shows also have a loyal and vocal audience poised to take the host's recommendation on products and services. Because Internet radio can deliver a highly specialized niche audience, you may be able to reach your target listener more effectively through these shows, as compared to interviews on traditional broadcast radio that may reach a larger total audience, of whom only a fraction are interested in your topic.

Paid Advertising

Some shows do not charge guests a fee to be interviewed, but actively seek paying advertisers or show sponsors. Shows may seek advertisers for several reasons. As previously mentioned, the host may be trying to recoup money paid to a network for the airtime. Some hosts have created a large enough following to be able to run their Internet radio show like a self-supporting business, where paid advertising and show sponsorship produces enough revenue to offset costs and provide a profit.

Assess these opportunities as you would for any paid advertising pitch. Here are some questions to keep in mind:

~ Can the show prove its listenership and downloads via an independent audit, or are you taking the host's word that people are listening?

~ Does the show provide a large enough targeted following to be worth the money? (Divide the ad's cost by the size of the audience and decide whether it's worth that amount of money per listener.)

~ Is the show archived via podcast so that people can listen later? If so, who has access to the recordings? (Some shows require a paid membership to access archives, while other post the recordings so that anyone can listen.)

~ What form does the ad take? Is it a banner ad, a graphic in rotation with other graphics, or a voice-over mention at the beginning and end of the show?

~ How long does the ad run? Will it be visible to everyone who visits the Website as well as to those who listen live and who download later?

If a show delivers a perfect fit to your target audience, it may be well worth the cost of an ad. Just be sure to do your homework before paying your money. Listen to several of the shows to assure that you're comfortable with the format and professionalism. Check out the Website and see whether other advertisers are presented attractively. Try listening to a few downloads to see how ads are exposed to those who listen later. If it still seems to be a good fit, make a commitment to a short period of time and then reassess when you've had a chance to gauge results.

Sight, Sound, and Motion on Internet Video

Web video should be a key component of your online marketing and PR strategy. Whether you're using professionally-produced clips or creating your own videos with a digital camera, Web video enables potential customers to see and hear you, giving them a greater level of comfort with you as a business resource.

Programs such as YouTube and AudioAcrobat have made it easier than ever to upload video to the Internet, embed short clips into blogs and Websites and share video via e-mail. Take advantage of these easy-to-use and inexpensive ways to add personality to your online presence.

You can't possibly meet all of your potential online customers in person. But good Web video provides a reasonable alternative. Customers like to feel that they are dealing with a real person, not just a Website. They want to get to know you beyond the words on your homepage. Enabling prospects to get a sense of who you are via Web video helps to decrease decision risk, which is the uncertainty a buyer feels about making a purchase. When a buyer feels he knows the merchant and has a level of trust, one level of decision risk has been eliminated, making it easier for a purchase to be made.

Online video also plays an important role in Internet PR. Many online press release distribution sites have an option to include links for Web video. Consumers and reporters like sight, sound, and motion to bring a story to life. Your News page on your Website can also become more interesting and lively by incorporating product videos, short snippets from recent Webinars or speeches, video tours, and even demonstrations. Even professionally-produced Web video can often be created at a fraction of the cost of traditional broadcast airtime. And with Web video, your "commercial" plays 24/7.

National airtime on broadcast TV costs millions of dollars, but compelling professional-quality video can be uploaded to YouTube for a minimal investment. An additional benefit of Web video is that people who click on your video actually want to see it. They will sit and watch it from start to finish. Compare this to consumer behavior during the average TV commercial when people go grab a snack, read a magazine, or catch up on chores.

Web video also provides a tool to bring your news to a national audience via traditional news organizations—such as CNN—that encourage readers to upload their own footage. During the crises in Haiti and Japan and the unrest in the Middle East, video coverage via cell phones and digital video cameras from regular people who were in the middle of the action often ended up on national TV. Shoot a good video or provide a clip that's related to a hot topic, and you might just end up on network and cable news—for free!

Results Reminder

Always keep your target audience in mind. If a show delivers your audience, it may be a good fit. No matter how popular it is, if it doesn't deliver your ideal audience, it's not worth your time or money.

The Rule of 30

Create a list of 30 shows with a good fit for your target audience. Check out their Websites, listen to their shows, and read the criteria posted by the host regarding the types of guests welcome on the show.

30

Exercises

1. Perfect your pitch. Create a short, clear statement of who you are and the nature of your expertise. Emphasize the value for the listener, and give the host a customized promise of what need you'll meet for his/her audience by being on the show.

2. If you need help perfecting your pitch, consider getting a media coach. I recommend Wayne Kelly (OnAirPublicity.com), who also has an awesome e-book on the subject.

19 Rock the World With Affiliate Marketing

If you spend much time looking up the term "online marketing," sooner or later you'll find the related phrase "affiliate marketing." Though affiliate marketing is a subset of online marketing, it is a viable and active part of many marketers' Internet strategy.

Affiliate marketing refers to the practice of enlisting the aid of other people and their Websites/opt-in mailing lists to sell your product. In a nutshell, you provide your affiliates with permission to sell your product (in return for a percentage of the profit), as well as with marketing templates and a customized Web link that enables you to track sales. In return, your affiliates promote your product to their opt-in mailing lists and Website visitors, as well as in their blogs and newsletters.

While affiliate marketing gurus often tout amazing success stories, proceed with caution. Some of the big successes with affiliates occurred before the market was quite so crowded, and there is always a first-mover advantage that is difficult for later entrants to replicate. Likewise, a good affiliate program requires thought, nurturing, and oversight in order to avoid problems and produce good outcomes. As individual states look at the potential of requiring sales tax for Internet transactions, affiliate programs face increasing complexity. Do your homework, but don't be scared away. Affiliate marketing still offers real potential for those who create worthwhile programs.

Create Your Affiliate Program Carefully

It may seem as though everyone on the Internet has an affiliate program. However, the real question is, How many are making money from their affiliates?

For a while, affiliate marketing was the new "get rich quick" Internet scheme. Many people, lured by the potential to make a 20 percent or better commission on products and services, signed up with anyone and everyone who had a program. They began to send out e-mails to their mailing lists with one offer after another. Inevitably, disillusionment set in. Where the product/service offered was high quality and a good fit for the audience, some affiliates were able to create a reliable stream of passive income. Often, the audience wasn't a good fit, or the product/service hadn't been carefully vetted by the affiliate, resulting in readers feeling barraged by spam. Affiliates who had spent years carefully building their permission-based e-mail lists saw subscribers opt-out. Products that weren't a good fit didn't sell. Enthusiasm waned.

A Formalized Version of Word-of-Mouth Advertising

The heart of a good affiliate program lies in word of mouth referral. If you have tried a product and love it, you want to tell your friends. The early affiliate programs were based on the concept of a "referral fee" for encouraging their personal contacts to buy programs/services they had used and liked.

I believe this is still the best form of affiliate marketing. If you have worked with a coach or purchased a product and loved the results, you may find that it's a good fit for your clients as well. If so, consider signing up for the vendor's affiliate program so that you receive a commission on the sales you generate on their behalf.

It gets a little murkier when it comes to products/services you haven't personally used. When you refer a vendor, you're not only recommending the product, but you're also, by default, saying something about their integrity, customer service, and ease of use. Referring products/services you haven't used can leave you in a sticky spot if the buyer doesn't have a good experience.

Likewise, it makes sense for you to reward your customers who refer business to you by creating your own affiliate program. Tread carefully when it comes to accepting affiliates who haven't actually been your clients. You want to be sure they aren't making inaccurate claims or using your link to spam people who aren't interested and haven't opted-in. You don't want your product or service associated with shady advertisers or junk e-mail.

Some people have made a full-time job out of being affiliates. They have become resellers, creating a one-stop shop for people searching for certain categories of goods or services. There's nothing wrong with having your product promoted by these folks so long as they are ethical and represent you with integrity. Do your homework before risking your reputation.

Qualities of a Good Affiliate Program

The best affiliate programs educate their affiliates on how to represent them and their products. They require affiliates to sign a statement that they will not engage in spamming anyone and will adhere to a code of ethics. You can limit the ability to become an affiliate to just your current and former customers, or accept anyone who wants to resell your product. However you go about attracting affiliates, it's wise to spell out how they may use your name, logo, and product names, and to do everything possible to assure that you are represented with integrity.

Good affiliate programs increase the chance for affiliates to succeed by providing training and marketing templates. These programs teach affiliates about the products and services they want to resell so that the products are represented accurately and marketed to the right audience. By creating marketing templates with the verbiage, photos and links you want your affiliates to use, you increase the chance that your product/service will be presented in the way you'd like it to be shown. The better educated your affiliates are and the more help you provide through easy-to-use materials, photos, and support information, the more likely it is that you and your affiliates will have a positive experience and make more sales.

If you decide to make your affiliate program a major part of your income, consider listing your program with a site such as CommissionJunction. CommissionJunction.com and similar sites act as marketplace where would-be affiliates can find affiliate programs, and companies offering affiliate programs can find enthusiastic affiliates. Many shopping cart programs also make it possible to create affiliate links that will track sales for a particular vendor through a unique URL. The ability to track sales from a particular affiliate's link is crucial to creating a workable affiliate program. Just remember that an affiliate program requires more than just links and tracking to be successful.

Be sure to consult a tax professional regarding your affiliate sales program. The issue of Internet sales tax is constantly evolving on both a national and state-by-state basis. Keep careful count of what you sell and what you make via affiliate channels so that you don't find yourself on the wrong side of the tax man. Even the rumor that particular states might enact Internet sales tax has been enough to make some online retail giants drop their affiliate programs in those states. Although sales tax may be new in the world of the Internet, it's certainly not new to other, long-established retail structures such as franchises, multi-level marketing programs and national chains who have figured out how to deal with it. Be sure you know your state's requirements, and keep an eye on emerging federal Internet law.

Results Reminder

A successful affiliate program requires a combination of education, reproducible marketing, and technology in order to meet the needs of the affiliate and the vendor.

The Rule of 30

Can you tap 30 of your most loyal fans to create the core of an affiliate program?

30

Exercises

1. Before starting your own affiliate program, investigate existing programs connected to reputable companies or experts. Sign up and see what it's like from the affiliate's point of view. Which programs provide education and marketing materials? Which leave you on your own to sink or swim?

2. Read up on affiliate marketing best practices. Be sure the book or article you're reading is recent because the Internet changes quickly

PR and Marketing Gold With Professional and Industry Media

20

Online PR and marketing aren't just about reaching reporters and consumers. Most companies find it helpful to promote themselves within their own industries. By including your profession or industry in the scope of your online PR and marketing activities, you heighten your credibility as an expert and position your business as a leader and innovator.

There are many potential benefits to promoting your company within your profession or industry. As you gain notoriety as an acknowledged expert, you're likely to be invited to speak at conferences and seminars. Not only can this create an additional stream of revenue, but it also provides excellent visibility for you and your firm, which can lead to the development of new client relationships. Likewise, being acknowledged within your industry as a leader and innovator can lead to invitations to serve on boards of directors, to award nominations, and to participation in think tanks and publication opportunities. Each of these opportunities further enhances your reputation, leading to more prestigious invitations.

Surprisingly, many business owners overlook their own profession/industry when it comes to online PR and marketing. Some fear that heralding their success will increase competition. That's unlikely to be the case, because anyone who is serious about competitive intelligence already knows who the leaders and innovators are. Others who promote actively to reporters and consumers feel suddenly shy within their own profession, as if developing visibility was akin to bragging. Promotion is a part of business. You're likely to miss out on opportunities if your colleagues don't recognize the strength of your achievements.

Reaching the Professional/Industry Media

Most industries and professions have a few key professional/trade associations. Those associations usually publish magazines or newsletters, hold annual conferences, and provide continuing education programs throughout the year. As organizations look for ways to decrease costs, an increasing number of the publications and programs are going online. This creates an additional outlet for your news releases, Web audio and video clips, and case studies.

Editors of trade and professional journals often despair at a lack of news from practitioners within their industries. They're looking for interesting news, guest bloggers, opinion pieces, articles, and case studies from leaders and innovators. They also want to showcase what's going on in the industry or profession, so news about awards, new products, honors, and expansions are all valuable to the folks who are responsible for filling journal pages with newsworthy information.

Most professionals simply don't take the time to cultivate relationships with the reporters and editors who cover their industry. Yet these reporters and editors are the ones tapped to put together conference and convention programming, suggest panelists and contributors to publications, and nominate leaders for awards. Your name isn't likely to come up in these discussions if you haven't made the effort to keep association contacts apprised of your accomplishments.

Whether you're an old hand or a newcomer with a fresh perspective, you can find a way to add value to the online discussion within your industry, and by doing so, enhance your reputation and the awareness of your firm.

Soft Sell Works Best

As with other media and online sites, focus on informing, not on selling. Promote yourself with an eye toward educating colleagues and advancing the dialogue. If possible, be entertaining as well as informational.

Position yourself as an expert who is willing to share and to help others grow. This requires coming with an abundance mentality instead of fear of scarcity. The scarcity thinker fears that enabling others' success leaves less for him. The abundance thinker believes that there can be more than enough for everyone by expanding the pie from which the pieces are cut. Help your colleagues bake bigger pies!

Don't be afraid to utilize the social media resources provided within the membership sites of your professional or industry association Websites. This can include forums, chat rooms, and message boards. Ask and answer questions, providing real value. Be sure your posts have your full name, company name, Web address and an e-mail address so people can follow up with you. When you become a regular contributor with consistently good ideas, you gain a reputation as an expert and a leader.

Consider taking an occasional banner or online ad within your trade/professional publication. This can show support and solidarity with the organization as well as making your company name and logo visible to everyone who visits the site. Depending on the size of the organization and whether it is regional or national in scope, pricing can be very reasonable compared to other advertising alternatives. Making an occasional splash, especially when it's linked to an anniversary, special event, or new product launch, can leave a lasting positive impression.

Make yourself available as a contributing expert for articles, interviews, and panel discussions. Suggest topics to the editors of the publication and Website, and offer to help make connections for them with other relevant experts. A good article in a trade publication can lead to an invitation to expand on the topic as a speaker at a national conference in front of thousands of people. This is a great example of how online PR can lead to offline opportunities for enhanced visibility. You'll see the best results when you consistently use online and offline PR and marketing to support each other.

Many professional organizations provide an online directory of their membership. Be sure that you earn the admiration—and not the scorn—of your fellow professionals by using your access to this directory responsibly. Never enter anyone's name into your mailing database without their opt-in permission. Don't send out broadcast e-mails promoting your company or your product. This kind of behavior qualifies as spam, even if you are a member of the organization, and may result being terminated from the site.

A better approach is to go through the member listings one by one and identify the people who look like a good fit, either as potential referral partners, or as potential partners to cross-promote or co-create products. Approach each person individually with a customized e-mail, mention that you are a fellow member of XYZ organization and tell them that you see some opportunities for you both to potentially refer business to each other. Ask for a short (15-minute) phone conversation to explore possibilities.

Many of the people you contact won't respond. That's okay. They may be busy, or just not interested. Move on. Of those who respond, some may be a poor fit, either because of personality or because their goals are not in sync with yours. A handful will be enthusiastic and will understand immediately what you're trying to do. These are the people to focus on. They will yield the greatest value and may turn into a long-time resource. I have gained many lucrative business partners with just such an approach, as well as colleagues who became personal friends. Years after my initial contact, we continue to pursue joint ventures, create co-branded products and refer each other for projects and speaking engagements. It's an investment that pays a worthwhile dividend!

Results Reminder

Be sure to include a strategic online PR and marketing outreach to your profession/industry as part of your overall publicity campaign.

The Rule of 30

Can you find 30 different ways (articles, blog posts, opinion pieces, case studies, forum posts, and so on) you can interact with your trade, professional, or industry publications and events?

30

Exercises

1. If you haven't already included your trade/professional/industry publications in your media list, be sure you add them now. Add organizations that are affiliated or related to your industry as well.

2. Take time to study these publications and their related Websites, online forums, and events. Look for ways that you can maximize the value by taking advantage of all the promotional opportunities available.

Social Media and Online PR and Marketing

21

Small business owners and professionals know that they should be on social media sites (such as Facebook, Twitter, and LinkedIn), but few truly grasp the opportunities for online PR and marketing—as well as personal networking—that these platforms provide.

Social media works best when it is part of an overall marketing strategy that uses many different marketing tools. Online PR and marketing are two tools that integrate very well with social media. Social media is primarily a personal networking opportunity. On Facebook and Twitter, the emphasis is meeting people you don't know and inviting people you do know as acquaintances to friend or follow you so that they can get to know you better. On LinkedIn, the focus is on reconnecting with people with whom you've had a business relationship and have lost touch, or deepening the business relationship you have or are building with other colleagues.

Though it's true that social media is a conversation instead of a one-way broadcast (a point lost on many of the people currently misusing social media), it is possible to announce news, upcoming events and significant activities within the framework of that conversation. The key is to approach social media with a light touch instead of a blatantly promotional push.

Facebook, Twitter, and LinkedIn: The Big Three

In today's world, it's inappropriate to add everyone you meet to your mailing list. But you can invite everyone you meet to friend or "like" you on Facebook and to follow you on Twitter. Even better, you can let people know what topics you'll be discussing on each of these sites and invite them to join in the conversation. What a great way to let prospects get to know you better and to develop a relationship with them as they move down your sales funnel!

When it comes to content, focus on value. Provide tips, ask questions, post surveys and results, even give short excerpts from your books or articles. You can also provide links to interesting articles you've read by other people, review business books that have been useful for you, or report on industry trends. The key is to provide a glimmer of your personality while also offering valuable information to your readers.

You don't want to make the conversation a hard sell, but it's okay to drop in news about you and your company. I suggest that your social media content be a 10 to one ratio—10 pieces of useful information that isn't about you and your company to one piece that is. Of course, if you're coming up on the last few days before a major event, it's all right to make a big deal about it. Just remember that people will tune out quickly if the information is heavily promotional and not immediately valuable to them.

Using Social Media as Part of Your Online PR and Marketing Strategy

You can create online events that include your social media sites, Website, and blog to create buzz. Develop a theme for your online event, and post unique copy on each of your platforms, giving readers an incentive to visit all of your sites. You can create free downloads, offer online-only specials, and feature a mix of real-time online interaction (such as being available live to answer questions on a blog or on Facebook) with material like articles, audio and video clips, and blog posts that have been prepared in advance. Use banner ads and Facebook ads to promote the online event and drive traffic. I create two online events each year and they have been fantastic ways to reach new readers and drive Web traffic without the cost and complexity of live events.

When you receive media attention, let your social media followers know. Post a link to articles, radio interviews, TV clips, videos or blog posts where you are featured. This builds goodwill with the reporter who interviewed you, because it drives traffic to the reporter's site. It also reinforces the perception of you as an expert, because you're in the media spotlight. And it creates an interactive experience for readers who have a chance to click and explore rather than reading a series of text posts.

Integrate social media into your online PR and marketing master calendar. If you're doing seasonal promotions on your Website, in your store or at your events, create a linked promotion online and in social media. Look at the seasonal or business cycle patterns in your business, and create themed content around those patterns to discuss topics that are uppermost in your target audience's minds.

Social media does its best work for you when it helps to reinforce and leverage marketing efforts in conjunction with a variety of other online and offline tools. So if you're sending out direct mail postcards, steer readers not only to your Website, but to a special offer on your Twitter or Facebook page. Provide an incentive to friend or follow you, whether that is access to online specials or the ability to be part of a great conversation.

LinkedIn works a little differently than Facebook and Twitter, because the emphasis is on deepening relationships with people you actually know. This requires a light touch for PR and marketing, similar to how you'd slip in news of an accomplishment or an award into a personal conversation. It's okay to use your status bar to let your LinkedIn connections know that you have a new book available, that a new product has launched, or that you're speaking at an event. Just don't bombard them with a non-stop onslaught of promotional messages. Be sure to acknowledge and celebrate your connections' triumphs, and recommend people whom you can honestly refer.

Another great way to keep yourself visible on LinkedIn without using a hard sell is by proactively connecting the people you know with each other when you see potential mutual benefit. The LinkedIn community also values expertise. Dive into the many interest groups and make valuable (but not self-promotional) contributions to the conversations going on there. Answer questions, provide answers, and help out. By doing this along with providing recommendations, you demonstrate an attitude of generosity and abundance that encourages people to reciprocate and to view you as a leader. LinkedIn has also added the ability to create business pages in addition to personal profiles. It's a new feature worth checking out.

Facebook ads are another option to promote your business, product, or book for very little cost. You purchase an ad and determine the demographics of the Facebook users who can see it. You can set daily and lifetime budget caps so that you know in advance how much the total campaign will cost. The goal is to raise visibility for your promoted item as well as to encourage people to click through to your related profile or fan page. Facebook also provides daily statistics to track impressions and clicks. A few hundred dollars can reach millions of eyeballs and result in thousands of click-throughs.

Social media becomes even more important to your online PR and marketing campaign when you realize that a growing majority of Facebook and Twitter users access their accounts via mobile devices such as cell phones. Mobile phone marketing is rapidly gaining traction in its ability to reach desirable consumers who are always on the go. When you are present and active on social media, you are also reaching these consumers via their mobile devices, so that they don't have to slow down and log in to read your message. For advertisers who want to reach today's never-sit-still consumer, the combination of social media marketing and mobile phone messaging is a powerful combination.

Google Adwords is another powerful tool in your online marketing and PR toolkit. Google Adwords enables you to create ads linked to the keywords consumers enter into the search engine. When the words linked to your ad are typed by the consumer, your ad appears in the "sponsored links" areas at the top and to the upper right hand side of the screen. Your link is the first thing consumers see.

The goal is to drive traffic to your site by matching you with the customers who are looking for what you offer. You write your own link copy and set your budget. Google Adwords even has a special service for local businesses to target consumers within the geographic area specified by the advertiser. Google uses its Keyword Tool to let you estimate the amount of searches for a particular term and the potential click-throughs each term might generate. It's a great way to raise your visibility and drive Website traffic inexpensively.

The Pros and Cons of Viral Marketing

Every marketer today hopes the campaign will go viral. They hope that the message will be so popular that readers will spontaneously forward the information to their personal networks, in effect, outsourcing marketing to the end users.

Be careful what you wish for. Viral marketing requires marketers to accept that once content, an image, or a video goes up on the Web, the person who posted it loses all control. As many celebrities, politicians, and abruptly terminated workers can attest, that's not always a good thing, especially if a spur-of-the-moment post is something you find yourself wishing later that you hadn't said.

Many long-time marketers struggle with the lack of control inherent in the concept of going viral. Career PR and marketing folks have been trained to restrict access so as to better measure results. In the old days, PR folks wanted to be the gatekeepers. Viral online marketing turns that paradigm on its head. In fact, all of online marketing and PR works on a contrarian principle that the fewer gatekeepers, the better, permitting reporters and consumers to find the information they want for themselves.

The real difference between viral buzz and word of mouth is scope. In the past, consumers had the ability to share their story with a much smaller group of people. A happy (or unhappy) customer could tell friends and family in and around the town where the merchant was located, but it was unlikely for the news to spread further. Today, viral buzz goes global in a matter of minutes. The great news is that consumers have the power to become world spokespersons for your company. Unless they've had a bad experience. Then the whole town, country, and world can hear about the customer's disappointment.

What do you do when, inevitably, someone posts that they've been unhappy with your company? Fight the urge to argue, pull down the post, or seek legal revenge. Unless the person has used abusive and obscene language, leave the post up. Respond calmly and put your customer service know-how on display for the world to see. Make every effort to set the situation right, even if you don't think you were in the wrong. When bystanders see how hard you are working to satisfy a disgruntled customer, your reputation rises. If the person making the complaint is unreasonable or nasty, sympathy shifts from the complainer to you, the wronged company.

Results Reminder

Make social media part of your online PR and marketing strategy to reach a large and targeted key audience.

The Rule of 30

Choose a 30-day period and make a social media push. Post every day, add new friends each day, take a Facebook ad, and invest in Google Adwords for your key search term.

30

Exercises

1. Use Google Keywords to generate a list of your top ten most relevant (and most searched) keywords.

2. Now use Google Adwords to estimate the cost of purchasing your top keyword(s) to put your results at the top of the page.

3. Use the same keywords when you create your Facebook ad.

4. Be sure to use the top most-searched keywords in all of your online press releases, blog posts, and social media entries.

Online Marketing and the "New" Media Revolution

22

"New" media refers to communication options via the Internet as well as mobile technology. It's new compared to traditional paper-based or broadcast options such as newspapers, magazines, radio, and TV. What's interesting is that much of the new media consists of "old" media reincarnated to an online format. Don't be fooled—this change is more than cosmetic. The real revolution is the change that occurred in the way people consume information.

I've already talked about the way the Internet changed the news cycle from an hour's worth of programming in the morning and at 6 and 11 p.m. to a 24/7 never-ending deluge. That shift dramatically increased the need for news, and created opportunities for your press releases and online marketing messages to be heard and repeated. But behind that opportunity lies the shift in consumer behavior. In the Internet age, consumers expect to get the information they desire when they want it served up in a way that's convenient to them.

That's a big change from demanding that people be in front of their TVs or radios at a particular time in order to get news. Welcome to the rise of the empowered online consumer.

As magazines and newspapers migrate online, the hunger for news increases. Online-only magazines can draw substantial readership. The same is true of blogs. The newspapers and magazines that continue to publish in paper often have Web versions with additional copy and commentary, plus social media sites and blogs. These sites present enormous online PR and marketing opportunities if you know how to take advantage of what they offer.

Make it Easy for Your Content to Be Used

Would you like to be quoted in newsletters and blogs that reach your target audience without even having to pitch the editors? Article directories such as EZineArticles.com can make that possible.

Sites such EZineArticles make it easy for bloggers, reporters, and e-publishers to grab fresh topic content from a variety of experts. You, the expert, post articles on the site. Bloggers and editors are permitted to use the content in the articles for free, subject to several rules: they must not edit or change the material, they must use the author's byline, and they must print the "resource box" at the end of the article which provides the author's links and information.

I've seen my articles show up in magazines and e-zines around the world by utilizing article directories. When your article is reprinted, you gain visibility to that publication's readers, and that article now turns up in search engine results to boost your rankings and increase your qualified inbound links. You gain a double benefit that lasts indefinitely, all for a few minutes' work posting your article.

Remember that you don't have to write brand-new copy for these articles. It's perfectly okay to re-use material you've created for your own newsletter or blog, or that was part of longer transcripts or presentations. So long as you wrote the copy and own the copyright, you can re-use it as often as you please.

If you've set Google Alerts to your name, company name, and product/book names, you'll automatically receive notification when your articles are re-used. (Sometimes editors will send you a courtesy note of thanks as well.) You can extend the benefit by using social bookmarking to let everyone see the article when it runs by adding it on sites like Technorati, Digg, and StumbleUpon. Social bookmarking sites are the virtual equivalent of the office bulletin board, where people who have found interesting tidbits used to thumbtack cartoons and articles with a sticky note that says, "Read this!" On social bookmarking sites, people share content they have found interesting with the world, sorted by category and topic.

When you bookmark one of your online articles, you're making it easier for people who are interested in your information to find what they need. You also benefit from increased search engine visibility, because every mention of your company online is searchable. Best of all, adding virtual bookmarks is free. (You can also bookmark Web video and audio, Websites, and blog postings.)

Don't succumb to the temptation of thinking online publications are somehow second class. The last few years have seen a rapid decline in the readership of traditional magazines and newsletters, with many long-time standards going out of business. In their place, a varied crop of online publications have sprung up. These present enormous online PR and marketing opportunity for businesses of every size.

Digital publications are also increasingly read by consumers from their mobile devices, such as smart phones, and tablet computers such as iPads. Not only can these prospective customers read your content on the go, but they can also click through live hyperlinks in the text to access extended content, such as your Website, associated Web audio and video, background information, photos, and more. They can pass your article along to their friends with "share" buttons that enable them to post content that interests them to social bookmarking sites and also to their own Twitter, Facebook and other social media pages.

QR (Quick Response) codes also make it easy for readers to find and access your online content. QR codes are the black and white boxes filled with a pixilated pattern. When a smart phone using the QR reader app (downloadable application) scans the QR code, it takes the person directly to a Web page for the company that posted the code. Instead of making them type in the URL, the QR code is a shortcut to take them to the precise page the owner of the code is promoting. QR readers can be downloaded from the iTunes App Store for free, or found online at a variety of sites. To create a code, you can go to Tag.Microsoft.com or do a Google search to find one of the many code generators available online.

You don't have to land an article in a major online publication to benefit. Constant Contact now makes it possible to add "share" buttons to e-mail newsletters sent by individuals and small businesses. Constant Contact users can also use a built-in link to Tweet a link about their new newsletter on their Twitter accounts. It's never been so easy to share interesting information—and if you're creating news people need to know, you stand to benefit from the trend.

Don't Overlook Online Ads

Many of these online publications accept advertising. Some provide featured links, which appear at the top of the page much like a private version of Google AdWords. Others utilize graphic ads, which may appear in a side column or as a banner at the top of the page.

When you find an online publication that interests you, check their online ad rates. Rates can be very reasonable. (Always be sure you know how large their audience is and how they document their readership). For a minimal investment, your Web designer can create an eye-catching interactive banner graphic that enables readers to click through to your Website or product page. The result? Highly motivated traffic funneled right to your site at an affordable cost.

Another plus with online advertising is the ability to track impressions (people who have seen the page) as well as click-throughs (people who actually click on the ad to go to your site). Don't be surprised that far more people see your ad than click through it. Impressions are important, even if the viewer isn't ready to visit your page just yet. The goal of PR and marketing is to keep your company constantly visible to your target audience (remember those 30 Magic Touches?) so that when the consumer is ready to buy, you are top of mind. Online advertising is another way to keep the visibility going.

Take full advantage of online capabilities when creating your banner or sidebar ad. Online ads can incorporate motion, which is a great attention-grabber. You can create your own version of a rotating billboard by having different images cycle, or have a Flash-powered mini-video add a moving image of your choice. If appropriate to your topic, humor or whimsy can appeal to customers who might otherwise ignore a "serious" ad.

As you browse the Internet, begin to pay attention to what other advertisers are doing. Don't limit yourself to what's being done within your profession or industry. Which ads catch your attention? What made you look—and read—the ad? Borrow what works, regardless of the nature of the business that used the technique, and find a way to apply it to your online ads. Taking an approach borrowed from another industry can make your ad stand out as fresh and different compared to your competition. The key to success on the Internet is continual, rapid adaptation and innovation!

A Few Thoughts About Squeeze Pages

"Squeeze pages" are almost synonymous with online marketing. They've been part of the online marketer's arsenal since the early days of e-commerce.

A squeeze page is devoted to providing a focused sales conversation to close the deal. You're most likely to find a squeeze page on the site of an online expert who is selling a proprietary system (usually a bundle of related products on a how-to business topic). Typically, a squeeze page is written like a conversation between the seller and the prospect, and it usually tries to overcome objections. Often, squeeze pages are peppered with written, audio, and video testimonials from satisfied customers. These testimonials go beyond general praise to cite specific, detailed results achieved through using the featured product or applying the expert's system.

A "buy now" link is prominently featured at several points throughout the squeeze page to take a convinced prospect directly to check-out. On the check-out page, it's common for the prospect to receive a bonus of some kind as an added inducement to purchase. This bonus usually comes in the form of extra downloadable material, and may feature downloads from a variety of partner-experts who have been recruited to participate in the promotion. The "buy now" landing page also provides additional testimonials and recaps benefits to keep the prospect hooked through the purchase process and to avoid buyer remorse that might cause the prospect to abandon the shopping cart without completing the purchase.

Squeeze pages are an online version of long-copy direct mail. If you've ever actually read the letter that comes with a fundraising solicitation, a timeshare advertisement, or a specialty collectible, you'll find squeeze page copy to be familiar. "Long copy" (as advertisers call it) does have a history of producing high sales, at least through traditional direct mail. Squeeze pages take the old direct mail concept into the online world via video, audio, and interactivity.

Although squeeze pages have been very successful for many of the first adopters of Internet marketing, there is some debate over how well the present techniques will continue to work in the future. Many of the original Internet marketing pioneers (or their marketers) were men who came from a traditional direct mail/advertising background. These squeeze pages take a very assertive hard-sell approach. These "old school" squeeze pages often refuse to disclose the price of an offer until the prospect has clicked through one or more links. The idea is that once you get people actively and repeatedly doing what you ask, their resistance to sales declines and they become more likely to buy. In the past, these types of pages have worked well.

Many sophisticated online consumers have voiced frustration with traditional squeeze pages. Some dislike the "hidden" prices and page designs that force someone to read all the way through an offer to get to the "buy" button. Now that squeeze pages are no longer a new idea, veteran consumers are burned out and have caught on to the trick. Many female consumers feel that the traditional approach is overly masculine and unnecessarily aggressive. Others dislike feeling browbeaten into purchasing. Due to questionable claims, federal regulatory agencies have also begun to take a closer look at squeeze pages that appear to guarantee results or profit. Some online marketers have been threatened with legal action stemming from too-good-to-be-true promises of success. (Ever notice why so many weight loss ads have a footnote that says "results not typical"? It's because of laws against false advertising and inflated promises. Those laws apply online as well as offline.)

A good squeeze page may increase your conversion rate (the number of Web visitors who actually purchase). Before creating yours, visit the sites of some of the top online marketers and see what you like (and don't like) about their squeeze pages. Note how they use audio, video, and testimonials. Outline their pages to better understand how they create value and tension. Learn from the squeeze pages of the masters, but never copy anyone else's text or offers (that's plagiarism).

Think twice about creating a squeeze page that tries to intimidate readers into making a purchase, and be wary of taking an approach that might turn off female buyers (men and women do react differently to sales tactics). Be absolutely sure not to promise inflated outcomes or to guarantee results and that you can verify testimonials if requested to do so. (It's a good idea to be sure that any specific dollar amounts or percentages cited in testimonials by your clients can be verified by the client, for your protection and for theirs.) Be persuasive, but be sure you're also honest and fair.

Results Reminder

Keep a piece of paper next to your computer, and jot down ideas about ads that caught your attention as you surf the Web.

The Rule of 30

Create a list of 30 e-zines and e-newsletters that are a good fit for your audience, plus several article directories that will help those e-pub editors find your content.

30

Exercises

1. Spend 30 minutes investigating article directories and the e-newsletters and e-zines that best reach your target audience. Read the rules and follow them carefully.

2. Check out the squeeze pages of leading online experts. Try to outline the squeeze page's structure, and make notes about what you like or don't like to give you ideas for your own page.

The Power of "Local" Online Media 23

Many people resist integrating online PR and marketing into their promotional mix because they see themselves as "local" businesses. Yet online PR and marketing can be intensely local, depending on how the strategy is focused.

True, your company may not be interested in wooing customers that are thousands of miles away, or perhaps you're unable to provide your service or product long-distance due to licensing restrictions or the tangible nature of what you're selling. But don't forget—the people in your local area go online every day to get information, and when your business is absent, you've taken yourself out of their decision-making process.

Creating a local-intensive online PR and marketing presence requires focus. It also requires understanding how to use online PR and marketing tools to reach a geographically defined audience. In addition, it requires that your content and online activities all underscore the local nature of your business in a way that converts the people in your geographic target area into customers.

The Local Side of the World Wide Web

So much as been made of the opportunities opened up by the Internet for companies to deal globally (or at least, outside their local market) that many companies don't realize that the Web has a local side as well.

Your neighbors and customers, as well as prospects in your geographic area, go online as part of their everyday routines. They read online newspapers and magazines, search for information with Google, shop from online retail and wholesale stores, and download books, music, and software. If your business isn't part of the range of information they see when they go online, you're missing out on sales.

Some business owners feel that by having a Website they've done what's necessary to attract their online neighbors. But most Websites are fairly static. Few businesses update their Websites with the frequency with which social media sites, online newspapers and magazines, or blogs add new information. Internet search engines favor recency and relevancy. That means that information bubbles to the top of search results when it is very closely related to the search term (thanks to keywords) and recently posted. The twin factors of recency and relevancy often work against Websites because most sites don't change frequently enough.

Here's where online PR and marketing can play a huge role in assuring that your business gets it share of attention from local customers.

Online PR about the local activities your company sponsors can help your business connect better with local customers. Does your company host special events such as educational seminars, workshops, or grand openings? Do you participate in community programs, such as sponsoring Little League or holding a charity food drive? Do you offer daily or weekly specials or have live entertainment? If so, these are all very locally focused reasons to post online PR.

Many companies send press releases to their local offline newspaper or to local paper magazines. True, some of these publications also have online related sites and some of those local press releases may find their way onto the Internet. But many companies forget to target their news to online-only local publications, which means they are missing out in two ways: they miss readers of the online publication, and they fail to derive benefit from the search engine hits on their name/topic.

You can also use online PR and marketing to cultivate a local audience by ensuring that the content you post has a very local focus. Make your blog, Website, and social media pages the go-to location for your friends, neighbors, and customers to see local news first. Create contests that encourage your neighbors and local patrons to send in photos of themselves, their kids, or their pets. You can bet that when their photo is posted they'll shoot off an e-mail to several hundred of their social media contacts and drive traffic to your site.

Capitalize on the local angle of your social media pages, blog, and Website by running your own online banner ads to highlight your company, products, and services. Use Facebook ads that target readers within a geographic area or with locally-focused keywords. Don't overlook paid advertising in online publications to reach local readers. Realize that you're also reaching consumers at their laptops and on the go as they read the publication—and see your ad—via mobile devices.

Mobile advertising is a growing element of online marketing. Many local companies have gone from asking customers for their e-mail address to asking for their mobile phone number—and permission to send coupons, event news, and updates via text messages. This can work especially well for entertainment providers, such as nightclubs and theaters, that benefit from customers making a spur-of-the-moment decision on what to do and where to go based on mobile advertising. Likewise, letting your customers know about a special deal, an online-only coupon, or a newly available hard-to-get product via text message can result in sales you'd otherwise miss. Sites such as AdMob and MakeMeSocial specialize in helping companies add text messaging to their online marketing mix.

Social Media Becomes a Local Resource

Google AdWords offers specialized services to target customers within a 20-mile radius from your business. AdWords permits you to add or exclude areas, and can integrate your targeted AdWords campaign with text messaging.

Facebook can serve as a showcase for your community activity. When you host an event that benefits a local charity or sponsor a local sporting team, promote before, during, and after the event with updates, photos, Web video, and testimonials. Encourage attendees to become part of an ongoing conversation. Many companies successfully use their Facebook page as an instantly updateable second Website to let their community know what's going on and to share information and updates.

Twitter has been used by local charities to mobilize volunteers for projects or to alert donors to immediate needs. Animal rescue groups and humane societies have used Twitter to match shelter animals with new homes. Schools have demonstrated Twitter's ability to alert parents to unplanned closings or to request badly needed supplies or last-minute parent volunteers. Businesses Tweet about their upcoming live entertainment, dinner specials, or daily discounts.

Twitter can also help you promote upcoming local events, share photos and video via links, and give your online press releases a broader readership as you tweet news and provide links to coverage you've received in local online publications. Your blog can also be an effective part of your online marketing program by sharing the story behind your achievements or by providing deeper insight into what's happening with your business, which deals and events are coming up, or the news of your industry as it impacts local customers.

Foursquare is an intensely local social media application that makes going about your business or going out for the evening a shared experience treasure hunt. Foursquare users use the site and text messaging to share their current location as they patronize businesses, retailers, and entertainment venues. They can become the "mayor" of frequently visited sites, and can gather their friends to join them on a spur-of-the-moment basis. Foursquare rewards users who are out and about in their local area—and the local companies they frequent benefit as well.

Groupon subscribers can sign up to get special online deals from local businesses. Subscribers indicate their local area and their willingness to receive e-mails and social media alerts to short-lived discounts from local merchants. Companies sign up to provide limited-time special deals that are only available via Groupon. In some cases, deals are only available if a specified number of people show up to claim it. Groupon makes bargain hunting fun and social while retaining an intensely local flair.

LivingSocial is another site that offers a daily deal from local businesses with up to 90 percent off the regular price. Once a subscriber buys the daily deal, he/she has the opportunity to forward the deal to friends, and if one of those friends also buys, the original customer gets the deal item for free. It's a fun way to publicize specials while encouraging customers to tell their friends about your company.

Yelp, Local.com, and Citysearch are other sites that capitalize on the concept of "local." Not only can they help others to find your company more easily (both online and in person), many of these new locally oriented sites also encourage customers to rate their recent experience. Don't let that scare you off. If you provide good service and a good product, you have reason to expect most of your ratings to be positive. Those that aren't positive provide valuable feedback for you to make improvements, and a highly visible arena in which to demonstrate your great customer service to woo back a less-than-thrilled former customer.

Your neighbors, customers, and prospects are online, and they respond to businesses that reach them where they spend their time. Customers also like getting relevant messages and discounts when they're on the move. Create your own highly local online PR and marketing strategy and reap the benefits!

Results Reminder

The success of your local online PR and marketing strategy depends on a combination of locally focused content, local-benefit incentives, and creative use of social media and online advertising designed for a local audience.

The Rule of 30

What are 30 local topics or locally focused announcements or deals you could promote to drive traffic online and offline?

30

Exercises

1. Investigate Websites such as Groupon, Foursquare, and LivingSocial to see what programs are available to businesses in your area. What other companies in your city are using these programs? Look at what they're doing and find ways to adapt those ideas to suit your business.

2. What special offers, discount prices, or live events do you offer that could be promoted and extended via online PR and marketing? If you're not currently doing anything, what could you create that would be relevant to your target audience?

Online Newsletters 24

In previous chapters, I've told you how valuable it is for you to make your news available to the editors of online publications, including newsletters. Without a doubt these vehicles can be very useful in spreading your news and raising visibility for your company. When you're featured in someone's e-newsletter, they're essentially introducing you to their opt-in list. It's like a trusted referral, and it helps you drive Web traffic and sell product.

What about your own e-newsletter? Are you communicating regularly with your customers and prospects?

Creating an E-Newsletter With Pizzazz

E-newsletters ideally are fairly short (no more than one or two pages) and offer a combination of tips and special offers or promotional information. For best results, avoid long, run-on newsletters. Create an informative mix of tips, short items, quotes, announcements, and photos with a focus on providing value to the reader. Because many business people review most or all of their e-mail from cell phones and iPads, short, snappy content is especially important.

Programs such as Constant Contact, AWeber, and Vertical Response offer a large variety of customizable templates to help you create professional-looking e-mail newsletters. Many programs also allow you to use custom-created graphics for a look that is entirely your own.

Look for an e-mail newsletter program that also has good list management capability to help you gather and organize your opt-in e-mail address database. For example, Constant Contact makes it possible to create and name your lists, avoid duplicates, and remove people who ask to be taken off the list. Making it easy for people to unsubscribe if they want off your list is not just good customer relations, but it also keeps you on the right side of anti-spam law.

E-mail newsletter programs can help you integrate social media with your e-newsletter for maximum marketing impact. Constant Contact makes it easy to tweet about your new newsletter on Twitter and adds buttons for Facebook and other social media sites to your newsletter to make it possible for your recipients to pass your news along to their friends and followers. Look for built-in ability for recipients to easily forward your newsletter to their own friends via e-mail. AWeber has a built-in tool to turn your blog posts into a newsletter, helping you get more impact for the time you invest writing content.

Sites such as Constant Contact also make it easy to create an opt-in box for your social media and Website to encourage people who visit your other pages to join your e-mail newsletter list. If you have multiple newsletters for different audiences, Constant Contact's software makes it possible to give subscribers a choice of which of your newsletters they'd like to receive.

Many e-mail newsletter programs enable you to utilize online surveys. People are curious, and they like to know what others are thinking. Including surveys and polls in your newsletter (and then reporting the results) can be a great way to involve readers. Likewise, today's programs also make it easy to include Web audio and video as well as photos.

Getting More From Your E-mail Newsletter

Be sure your e-mail newsletter focuses on reader value rather than hard-sell pitches. Most of your content should provide information and tips, along with a featured offer or event invitation from your company. Avoid sending e-mail newsletters too frequently. Most companies do well with a monthly format. Some utilize a very short weekly tip or motivational quote along with one or two brief links to their own products or events.

Engage your reader by making your newsletter interactive. Give them a reason to click on links to see videos, hear audios, and read more beyond the short tip that's posted. Include polls and surveys. Give readers incentive to visit your Facebook page, Twitter feed and blog by mentioning the topics you've recently covered or will talk about soon. If you're promoting an upcoming event, include a link to the event sign-up page. Promoting a "special of the month" product or service? Be sure there's a "buy now" link handy to make it easy for readers to purchase.

Don't reprint your press releases in press release format, but do report your news, awards, upcoming programs, and participating in community and industry events. Be sure to include your own ads for products or events. If you have something big coming up, add a special banner ad to get attention. It's your newsletter; make it work hard for you.

Today's e-mail marketing programs also include tracking. Take the time to review these reports, because they will give you valuable information about how your readers are responding. If you see a lot of people opting out, you may be sending information too often, or you may not have a good match between your content and your readers' true interests. Are people clicking to open your newsletter? That's a good sign, but it may not tell the whole truth about the number of people who are actually reading the newsletter, because many people can preview an e-mail without clicking to open it. Look at your report to see how many people are clicking through on the links you provide. This will give you insight into which offers and what kinds of information are of greatest interest.

Building your opt-in e-mail newsletter list is an essential part of your online marketing strategy. Offer a free, downloadable bonus item on your Website and on your social media sites. This might be an article, white paper, case study, tip sheet, or quiz. Make it clear that receiving the free bonus item also includes a free subscription to your monthly newsletter, with the ability to unsubscribe at any time. Change your downloadable bonus offer every few months to keep it fresh and to entice new visitors to subscribe.

Ideally, you want to build a list of people who like what you have to say and have given you permission to stay in touch with them via e-mail. Never purchase or borrow an e-mail list compiled by someone else. Sending mass e-mails to people who did not request to hear from you is spam and it can reduce your businesses' credibility and even get you dropped from your e-mail provider. If you want to reach someone else's e-mail newsletter audience, work out an arrangement for that person to feature an article with your by-line, or run an ad with an affiliate link to your product. You gain credibility by being recommended by the list owner, and you keep yourself out of trouble.

Wondering where you'll find the time to write and create your e-mail newsletter? Many companies hire a virtual assistant to help with writing and laying out their e-mail newsletters. A virtual assistant is someone who provides administrative skills as an independent contractor working from a remote location. You can find quality virtual assistants on sites such as Elance.com and Guru.com.

E-mail marketing is very valuable part of a successful online PR and marketing strategy. Today's tools are inexpensive, easy to use, and very customizable, making it possible to create professional results within the reach of any small business or professional.

Results Reminder

Your e-mail newsletter is an essential tool in your online marketing and PR strategy. Be sure you integrate it with your press releases and special offers while respecting your reader's time and interests.

The Rule of 30

Check out 30 e-mail newsletters from other companies in your industry and from thought leaders outside of your profession. What appeals to you? What doesn't? Make a list of the best features to adapt to your own newsletter.

30

Exercises

1. Spend 30 minutes reviewing the tutorial for your e-mail newsletter provider and take the online tour. Get to know the templates and extras available to you.

2. Look at your existing printed or e-mail newsletter. Can you apply the tips from this chapter to make your newsletter work harder for you?

Using 25 Teleseminars and Webinars

In today's busy world, it's become more difficult for business owners and professionals to spare the time away from the office to attend conferences and take classes. Teleseminars are classes offered via audio, often over conference call lines. Webinars add a visual component, which can be a slide show, a shared white board, or even live Internet. Together, teleseminars and Webinars provide a great way to host free or fee-based live events for attendees across town or around the world. They're a powerful addition to your online PR and marketing efforts.

The Nitty-Gritty of Teleseminars and Webinars

Events are a great way to promote your business. When you hold educational programs, you showcase your expertise and increase your credibility as an expert and a leader. By educating users, you create demand for your products and services. Not only that, but events are newsworthy, creating a reason to send out press releases (and to post them online), potentially landing your business in the newspaper and in online publications. Events can help you build your opt-in list, and can be the gateway to profitable back-of-the-room sales. If you've got a hot topic, prospects and customers may be excited to attend and learn, deepening their relationship with you.

Virtual events mean that you can host the program from anywhere: your office, home, hotel room, or even your car, in a pinch. Your attendees have the same flexibility. Neither you nor your attendees have to rearrange the whole day to accommodate the program or commute. That's a real bonus—the gift of time.

There is a downside to live events. When you hold an in-person program at a hotel or other physical location, you pay for the facilities, the audio-visual equipment, and food and beverage for attendees. Even if no one shows up, you owe the location for the rental of its space. An in-person event also requires your attendees to take time away from the office, commute to the location, find (and possibly pay) for parking, and maybe even pay for their lunch.

Teleseminars and Webinars enable you to host live or recorded events without the expense, risk, and complexity of in-person programs. Attendees also like the convenience of participating without needing to leave the office, saving time and money. Today's technology makes it easy and inexpensive to create online events that can attract a global audience. It's also easy to record your teleseminars and Webinars so that attendees can listen at their convenience, or so that you can sell the audio and/or video as an online product.

To create a teleseminar, you need a topic, enough content to fill a half hour or an hour, and the ability to invite attendees to join in on a conference call. At one time, only larger businesses could afford conference lines. Now, programs such as FreeConference.com, FreeConferencePro.com, and FreeConferenceCalling.com make it possible for you to host hundreds of attendees on a conference line at no cost to you.

Look for a conference call site that offers the additional features you need to produce a high quality teleseminar. Many of these features are also free. For example, call sites offer the ability to schedule calls months in advance and to send e-mail invitations to attendees. Some sites enable you to record an audio greeting. For a fee, many sites make it possible for you to record the call, or if you already subscribe to a site such as AudioAcrobat.com, you can use it to record without incurring extra costs.

Free conference call sites don't charge the host for use of the line. However, most of these sites provide a call-in phone number which may incur long distance charges for your attendees. To get an 800 number assigned to your conference, there's usually an extra fee. Think before you pay for an 800 number. A growing number of business people have free long distance calling from their cell phones or landlines, and many people use Skype or other VOIP services that also offer free long distance. Let your attendees know that the dial-in number may incur long distance charges depending on their individual phone plan, and suggest they call in with Skype.

A Webinar adds a visual component to your virtual event. With a Webinar, attendees log into an online platform that enables them to see a slideshow, watch the host draw on a shared virtual whiteboard, or share photos or Websites in real time. Webinar software can be relatively inexpensive and easy to use, but it isn't free. Sites such as GoToWebinar.com offer an inexpensive option that enables you to reach hundreds of attendees at one time. Sophisticated programs from Adobe and Cisco provide a wider variety of features but are also much more expensive.

Getting Online PR and Marketing Benefit From Your Virtual Events

You can use all of your online PR and marketing tools to promote your virtual events just like you would promote an in-person program. As a first step, send out press releases to online and traditional publications and post the event announcement on your own Website. Be sure your press release is keyword-rich to make it findable via search engines.

Virtual events can also be listed on sites such as Conference Call University (*www.CCULearning.com*) that post a list of upcoming events. Don't forget to mention your virtual events on your blog and in your e-mail newsletter. Of course, you can also utilize offline marketing such as flyers in your store or office and postcard invitations if you desire.

Tie your virtual events into your social media platform. You can create a business fan page for your event and develop a Facebook ad to drive traffic to the registration link. Constant Contact has an event marketing feature that enables you to tie your e-mail newsletter directly into a customizable event promotion page just for your seminar or workshop. Constant Contact's event marketing feature also makes it easy to set up the page, promote the event, manage registration, and track responses.

Tweet about your upcoming event on Twitter, let your contacts on LinkedIn know about the program, and post information on the members-only sites for your professional and industry associations. On both Facebook and Twitter, make an effort to personally invite your friends and followers who are a perfect fit for the upcoming event.

You can also create a short Web audio or video about the upcoming event, a five-minute "free sample" to give potential attendees who are undecided or who don't know you well a chance to get a feel for your style and expertise. Of course, you can share the video via YouTube and share both audio and video via links on all your online platforms.

Think about how you want to "product-ize" your teleseminar or Webinar before the event. Many event organizers offer audio recordings of an event after the fact for a fee. You might create a downloadable handbook from your slide show along with note sheets to add extra value, and sell the audio plus handbook as a package.

Your opt-in list of people who have inquired or signed up for your virtual events can become your go-to list of invitees if you decide to create an in-person extended seminar, workshop, or retreat. Be sure you stay in touch with them about other virtual events you're hosting and nurture your online relationship to bring them further down your sales funnel and turn prospects into customers. Don't forget to offer snippets from the audio and/or video online and via social media to attract new visitors to your site.

Teleseminars and Webinars can be powerful additions to your online PR and marketing strategy. Online events provide an affordable, easy-to-manage way to introduce your expertise to new prospects. You can also create a new revenue stream through attendance fees and sell the recording as a product. Look for ways to utilize all of your online promotional tools to promote your virtual events and build valuable connections.

Results Reminder

Teleseminars and Webinars are a great way to reach an audience that might never be able to see you present in person, but who are very willing to buy your products or services online.

The Rule of 30

Create a list of 30 organizations, online sites, or e-learning programs where you would be a good fit as a teleseminar or Webinar presenter.

30

Exercises

1. What live presentation might lend itself well to presentation as a teleseminar or Webinar? How might you need to adjust your speaking style to address an invisible audience?

2. Spend some time attending teleseminars and Webinars related to your field to see who the stars are, what the style is, and how the material is presented. Factor this information in as you create your own presentations.

Online Events for Speakers and Authors

26

Online marketing and PR create a global stage where speakers and authors can connect with an audience they might never meet in person. At a time when few publishing houses will underwrite book tours and many speakers pay their expenses themselves, online marketing creates low-cost, high-impact ways to reach more people while spending time and money more effectively.

Virtual Campaigns Get Tangible Results

Today's virtual marketing campaigns have an array of effective tools which can be combined in unique and creative ways to reach a huge, highly targeted audience. Authors have books to sell, and speakers often have information products for sale. Online marketing can be a powerful way to connect with far more potential consumers than might be reached by book signings or in-person speaking engagements.

For example, an author can create a Facebook ad campaign with the book's cover graphic. Facebook allows users to set both daily and lifetime budget limits, so you're always totally in control of what you're spending. You can also choose the age, interests, and other demographics of who gets to see your ad, so it's only going to the people who are most interested in what you have to offer. Your ad enables the reader to click through to your Webpage or to your Facebook page. For a very small budget, you can create an ad that is seen by millions of people (called "impressions"), and that generates hundreds, thousands, or tens of thousands of click-throughs to your Facebook page or online offer.

Google AdWords works in a very similar way, only your ad appears on Google, not on Facebook, and the ad only appears when someone uses one of the keywords you specify in their search. You set your budget, pick your keywords, and pay only when people click on your ad. Put the two together, and it's possible to reach millions of people who fit your target audience profile for just pennies a day.

Speakers may also want to time an "e-mail blast" to event planners via Espeakers.com or other speakers' bureaus to coincide with their Facebook or Google ad campaign for maximum impact. Authors can get more visibility out of a physical book tour by timing their personal appearances to happen at the same time as their Google or Facebook campaign. Leverage social media by using Twitter and LinkedIn to draw attention to your online campaign as well. If your marketing includes elements such as direct mail, e-newsletters, or ads in electronic or traditional publications, get the most bang for your buck by having all of the elements in play at the same time.

The Magic of Online "Tours"

Whether you're a speaker or an author (or both), one thing is true: your time is limited. No matter how well known you are, you've only got 24 hours in a day. And for all but the very pinnacle of authors and speakers, budgets are limited. Many events that used to pay expenses for speakers to attend now expect speakers to cover their own travel costs. Few publishing houses will sponsor authors on a physical tour. Even if events and publishers did pay to put you on the road, it's just not possible to be at every event, every bookstore, or every trade show.

That's where the magic of online "tours" comes in. For an author, an online tour means setting up guest exposure on a multiple blogs, Websites, Internet radio shows, podcasts and social media sites to talk about your book and its benefits. For speakers, a tour of similar online venues helps you increase your visibility, provide a short "sample" of your style and expertise, and make it easy for interested individuals to connect with you to book you for their events.

To set up an online tour, find blogs, podcasts, Internet radio shows, and other sites dedicated to your type of book or topic of expertise. Get a feel for the kind of content they provide and see if you can determine their audience. Aim for getting at least seven sites lined up for your tour (that gets you through a full week).

Think about how you can publicize your online tour. Of course you'll mention it on your own Website, social media pages, and e-newsletter. You can also post a press release on the free and paid PR distribution sites. Add up how many friends/followers you have on social media as well as your opt-in list and your media distribution list. Create a Facebook or Google ad to sweeten the deal. Now you have a powerful win-win to offer to your potential tour partners. They win from having you publicize the tour because you'll introduce their site to all your contacts and send them new traffic. You'll also give them something new and interesting to talk about, which helps them attract and keep readers/listeners. And you'll be mentioning your partner sites in all your PR (using both free and paid online distribution sites), which boosts your partners' visibility and increases their search engine hits.

Write a personal e-mail to the owner of the blog or podcast site you'd like to partner with, and introduce yourself. Let the owner know that you are planning an online tour and ask if they'd be interested in participating. Give a quick outline of the benefits you can provide in exchange (as described in the previous paragraph).

Don't be discouraged if some of the people you contact don't want to participate or can't do it at the time you need to run the tour. If it's just an issue of timing, keep them in mind for the next tour. If they're not interested, go on to the next person on your list. Remember that your partners don't need to be huge or famous, they just need to have a solid, loyal following who are a good fit to be your customer.

Online tours can make it possible for you to make a "local" appearance in places far from where your budget allows you to appear in person. You can build a wide following, and acknowledge existing customers and fans by coming to their "neighborhood" and create an international presence—without leaving your office.

See Your Name Everywhere

Books get sold and speakers are chosen to speak in part because of name recognition. It's the "Oh, I've heard of him/her" process. Readers wander the aisles of a bookstore (or online bookseller) looking for something to read. They spot a book with an interesting cover, and the "Oh, I've heard of him/her" process kicks in. Name recognition plus a good cover and an intriguing excerpt make the sale.

Likewise, event planners may sift through hundreds of speaker applications for a popular event. You may have a great speaker sheet, work with a top bureau, use a wonderful headshot and have highly relevant topics, but there's nothing like the "I've heard of him/her" factor to get your application pulled out and put on the fast track.

All of your marketing activities contribute to building name recognition, but online marketing and PR is one of the fastest ways to become the person everyone seems to be talking about. When you have a Facebook ad; show up at the top of the search rankings with Google Adwords; appear on a dozen or so blogs, podcasts, and Internet radio shows within a short period of time; have an active social media presence on Twitter, Facebook, LinkedIn, and your own blog; send out an e-newsletter; take a few carefully chosen banner ads on inexpensive but relevant sites and have thousands of search results, people see your name over and over again, leading to the impression that you're hot stuff. Every teleseminar or Webinar you participate in, each online event and guest blog, every online press release and YouTube video builds your name recognition.

If everyone appears to be talking about you and you seem to be everywhere, others want to jump onto the bandwagon. You're no longer an unknown; after all, you're at the top of the Google results for your topic! Even when a bookstore manager or event planner can't quite remember where they've seen your name before, it's much better for it to ring a bell than for them to say, "never heard of him/her."

Save a Bundle With a Virtual Portfolio

Not too long ago, speakers and authors had to spend hundreds or thousands of dollars to print glossy materials to be sent out to event planners or book stores in order to book presentations or appearances. These kits often included CDs or DVDs to show the presentation style of the author or speaker and to add credibility to their claims of expertise.

Thanks to online marketing and PR, you can save all that money with your virtual portfolio, which is very similar to the online press kit we discussed earlier in the book. Instead of a DVD, provide links to videos you've posted on YouTube showing how you look in action presenting or at a book event. Include an audio clip of yourself reading from your book or welcoming event planners to your site. Add links to your social media sites, blog, and recent online appearances or virtual tours.

Mention where you've been a blog or podcast guest, been featured on Internet radio, or had an article picked up on a website or e-zine. Add sight and sound to your testimonials by having delighted readers, event planners, or program participants record their comments with Web audio or digital video. Add your book covers, photos of your information products, or even photos of the covers of program booklets which featured you as a recent speaker.

Now instead of a flat, boring promotion kit, you're providing a multi-media experience to introduce event planners, book store managers, or speaking scouts to you with sight, sound, and motion. And you've also saved a huge amount of money on printing, storage, shipping, and postage!

Results Reminder

Visibility builds the perception of credibility and expertise.

The Rule of 30

For 30 days, set your Google Alerts to track authors, experts, and thought leaders in your field. Where are they showing up on media?

30

Exercises

1. Identify 15–20 blogs and Internet radio shows that focus on your topic. Then look at your calendar and pick one or two seven-day periods where you could do an online tour. Be sure the dates are several months in the future to permit planning.

2. Develop a theme, a catchy title, and a business goal for your online tour. Create a win-win pitch to the bloggers and radio hosts, and then pitch your tour! Offer each participant a unique day and unique content, and let them know how you'll be promoting the tour to drive traffic to their site.

3. Add Facebook or Google ads to your online tour for extra impact. Investigate keywords that are closely aligned with your topic, and see what you can do within your budget. You might be surprised!

4. Don't forget to add online PR to your online tour mix. Be sure to promote your tour with releases posted on free and paid distribution sites. Start by creating a list of those sites (if you haven't already done so).

Basic E-Commerce Ties Promotion to Payoff

27

The goal of online marketing is to sell products through the Internet. In order to do that, you'll needs an online shopping cart. Online shopping carts are services that make it possible for you to list products and services for sale, accept online payments, and provide other important merchant services.

First, Show Me the Money

Before you commit to any shopping cart program, think about what you need from your cart. How will you accept payment?

First, determine whether your volume of transactions justifies having a merchant account. A merchant account enables you to take credit cards directly over the Web. Without a merchant account or an intermediary service, you won't be able to do business over the Internet, because you can't accept cash or checks.

You can create a merchant account through your bank or though one of the many services that specialize in credit card sales. Merchant accounts usually enable subscribers to rent/purchase a wireless credit card reader. This makes it possible for you to accept credit cards during in- person events as well as through your online shopping cart. On the down side, traditional merchant accounts are expensive, charging a monthly fee and a per-transaction surcharge that may exceed the sales of a beginning retailer.

Square is an alternative to the traditional merchant account. Square is free to join (*www.Squareup.com*). As of the writing of this book, the Square credit card reader is also free. Square provides a small card reader that's the size of a postage stamp with a plug to connect to a smart phone through the headphones jack. The Square app can be downloaded for free from iTunes or from the Square Website. Instead of a monthly fee, Square charges a low per-transaction fee. It also provides the ability to accept a credit card number without swiping the card through the card reader. Square charges a slightly higher per-transaction fee for cards that are keyed in instead of swiped through. Square provides a very viable alternative for companies that have a relatively low transaction volume or that may not use a card reader every month. It's easy to use, secure, and at the time of this writing, works anywhere within the continental U.S. (Square says they are working to make Canadian and other international transactions available soon.) To use Square, the merchant must have either a smart phone or a tablet PC (such as an iPad) and have access to secure WiFi.

If you are new to online commerce, you may want to begin with PayPal. PayPal is an online service that allows you to accept credit card payments without requiring you to have a merchant account. Instead, PayPal creates a buffer between the merchant and the buyer, safeguarding the purchaser's card information. The buyer creates an account that stores his/her card information. Using the PayPal interface, a buyer can purchase by using the e-mail address linked to the account.

However, buyers can only pay with PayPal if the merchant is also signed up with the service. And, merchants can only get paid if their intended buyer is a PayPal user. It is also possible for a PayPal user to pay directly from a bank account, and payments can be direct deposited into the merchant's bank account. PayPal is free to buyers but charges a transaction fee for sellers.

A Cart of Your Own

Now that you've decided on how to accept payments, it's time to shop for shopping cart programs.

Online carts vary tremendously in cost, ease of use, and flexibility. Ideally, you want a program that has capacity for you to grow without being prohibitively expensive for your transaction volume.

1ShoppingCart.com is a program popular for its user-friendly attributes. There are many other programs to choose from; just be sure to investigate cost and capabilities before investing.

At a minimum, an online shopping program should enable you to do the following:

~ Accept some form of online payment (ideally, several types of credit cards plus PayPal or a similar online money transfer program).

~ Offer a variety of products.

~ Set prices and edit descriptions for your products.

~ Deliver your downloadable products as part of the purchase process.

~ Notify you via e-mail when a purchase has been made.

~ Track applicable sales tax.

In addition to the basic functions, you'll find it helpful if your cart can also:

~ Handle multiple payments (enabling you to offer payment plans).

~ Accept "affiliates," resellers who promote your products in exchange for a percentage of sales.

~ Create autoresponders to continue the conversation with buyers by offering follow up messages via e-mail.

~ Provide you with options for how your "buy" link is presented and how your digital products are delivered.

~ Create coupon/discount codes.

Many template programs, such as Citymax, come with their own shopping cart functionality. Though convenient, these programs often have limited capabilities. If you outgrow the template program and want to change your Web hosting, you'll also have to rebuild your shopping cart. These built-in programs often do not offer enhanced capabilities such as the ability to accept affiliates or process payment plans. Think ahead to determine what range of functions will best serve your business during the next few years.

Integrating Your Cart Into Your Online Marketing

Once you have the ability to process online transactions, it's time to crank up the marketing engine.

Be sure everyone who visits your Website knows you offer the ability to buy online, Use the navigation bar to offer a page for "Products" or your very own online store. Feature photos of your products on your home page, and link directly to your "buy" link for shopper convenience.

You can use your "buy" link anywhere you can embed a link. Consider including a link in your e-mail newsletter, your blog, or in your Facebook ads. You can tweet your "buy" link on Twitter. If the link is long and cumbersome, use a free service, such as tinyURL.com to make it easy to embed. You can also use HTML to "hide" the URL in a text link, such as "buy now," which is much more appealing to readers.

Having e-commerce capabilities makes it possible for you to send people to your Website to make a purchase, extending your sales opportunities. During in-person and online networking, you can refer to your product page, making it easy for your audience to buy. Even better, your online store is open 24/7, enabling you to earn money while you sleep!

Results Reminder

An online shopping cart makes your Website into a store that never closes, available to a global audience.

The Rule of 30

Where are 30 opportunities to promote your online store or use your link?

30

Exercises

1. Visit a number of online retailers and pay close attention to their shopping carts. Realize that huge merchants, such as LL Bean or Amazon, handle a volume of transactions that require more advanced cart features than what you are likely to need.

2. Visit the online stores of other businesses that are in your industry, to see what the norm is. Be sure that you are also looking at the carts of businesses that are approximately the same size as your own in order to make a fair assessment of features and functionality.

28 Hybrid Online Tools Bring the Pieces Together

As you're creating your online marketing and PR strategy, look for tools that make it seamless to create and distribute multi-media programs. Think beyond the written and printed word. Today's online audience expects sight, sound, and motion from social media and blogs, from e-newsletters and from press releases.

Fortunately, many new programs make it easy for you to incorporate multi-media elements and ties to social media. As you evaluate tools, look for those that have built-in connections to social media and multi-media functionality to make your online marketing time go twice as far.

The Role of E-mail in a Social Media World

Has social media killed e-mail? Hardly. Though Facebook has a larger "citizenship" than the population of the United States, and sites such as Twitter and LinkedIn have tens of millions of users, e-mail remains the king of modern communication.

E-mail is at the heart of business and personal communication in the modern world. This means that e-mail must be a vital part of your online marketing and PR strategy in order for you to reach your widest audience and to reinforce your message.

Your opt-in list is the blood of your marketing program. This permission-based list enables you to stay in regular contact with people who already know you and like your product. It's your opportunity to keep the relationship warm with your regular consumers and to stay connected to your hot prospects. It's also an ongoing conversation to which you can invite everyone you meet.

Fortunately, e-mail has moved far beyond the early days, when people sent out text-only messages. Today's e-mail tools now incorporate a sophisticated combination of multi-media, social media, and tracking capabilities to turn your e-mails into a more personal conversation.

Constant Contact is a great example of a newsletter tool that has expanded capabilities to seamlessly incorporate many valuable capabilities. In addition to having a variety of easy-to-customize templates and robust features as an e-mail marketing system, Constant Contact now integrates online survey capabilities, event promotion, document archiving, content storage, and connection to social media. They are continually working to make it easier to embed video and audio. Built-in linkages to Facebook, Twitter, and other social media networks make it easy for users to alert their followers to the release of a new newsletter, and for readers to share the newsletters with their own followers, turning a great newsletter into a viral phenomenon. Because a majority of small business owners access most or all of their e-mail via their mobile phones, your e-newsletter becomes a form of mobile advertising when it can be accessed by users on the move.

Talk Fusion is another tool that makes it easy to create and share "video postcards" that incorporate text along with Web video and audio. These sight/sound/motion greetings leap off the screen, creating an intimate, personal conversation. For a touch of whimsy, consider the cartoonish animated figures you can create and customize in your own video (with your own voice) at Xtranormal.com.

Creating this in-person connection even when you can't be physically present is essential in today's online marketing world. Realize that your potential customers prefer to receive their information in different ways. Some people are heavily focused on the written word. Others learn primarily through audio. Still others need to watch in order to learn, and another group learns best by participating.

When your e-mail marketing incorporates multi-sensory content, you are making it possible for the recipient to experience your information in the format he or she likes best. There is something for everyone—sight, sound, and participation through live surveys.

Your target audience also receives reinforcement through sensory channels that may be secondary to his/her preferred mode of communication. So for example, for a person who learns best by reading, audio, video and participation via survey serve to reinforce the message and boost retention. Your message has the best chance of being heard, understood, and retained when you utilize all the senses.

Nearly all of the press releases and media pitches today are done via e-mail. Providing easy links to audio and video helps a radio host, TV producer or talk-show assignment editor determine whether you will be a good fit. Your ability to connect via video and audio lets the media see you in action, helping them to make the decision whether to cover just your business, or to also cover you. When the media decides that you are a good fit, you begin to move beyond product marketing into creating a platform for yourself and for your business.

More Hybrid Online Tools You Should Know

Doubleclick For Publishers (DFP) Small Business is a way for smaller publications that sell online ads to manage, program and track their ad inventory. DFP Small Business, a subsidiary of Google, provides a toolkit to help online advertisers track and deliver their ads, manage and forecast their ad availability, and provide detailed reporting. Using DFP Small Business, online publishers can choose the options that will sell the ad to the best available bidder at the highest price. DFP Small Business is linked to Google AdSense and to non-Google ad networks.

Ringleader Digital, Jumptap.com, Google AdSense, MakeMeSocial. net, and even AT&T are just some of the companies that have jumped onto the mobile phone advertising bandwagon. Mobile phones are attractive because customers carry them everywhere. With "smart phones" that are both phone and Internet browser, an increasing number of cell phone users consult applications on their phone to choose dining, entertainment, lodging, and other services. Depending on your type of business, mobile phone ads may make sense for you to consider.

Another form of mobile advertising comes in the form of "apps"—applications—on iPhones, iPads, and other "smart" phones. Apps make it possible for users to read magazines, access services, and easily connect with their membership sites without having to go through an Internet browser. Apps can also provide games, productivity tools, and easy access to branded services. In some ways, they are the modern equivalent of passing out advertising specialties, only these "tchotchkes" are interactive.

A growing number of sites make it possible for small businesses to afford to create custom, branded apps. Just like trade show exhibitors have given away calculators with their logos imprinted on them in hopes that every use will remind the user of the company, so branded apps maintain the same kind of visibility to a new generation. Check out IMSMB.com, Biznessapps.com, Libsyn.com, and similar sites; prices for app development, hosting and management vary.

Hybrid online tools enable you to personalize your marketing and PR, bringing a human, face-to-face focus that engages the customer and extends your relationship with prospects. Today's tools are more comprehensive than ever before, and also easy to use. Take advantage of these powerful programs that help you integrate a personalized touch with the full capabilities of the Internet.

Results Reminder

Hybrid tools allow your ideal customers to access your content when, where, and how they find it easiest and most convenient to do so.

The Rule of 30

Read 30 e-newsletters. What do you like? What don't you like?

30

Exercises

1. If you don't own a smart phone, or use your phone only for voice calls, get a "power user" to show you what an iPhone, iPad, or Droid can really do.

2. Once you've had your introduction to smart phones, check out the business apps available via your phone's app store and other locations. See how other companies are using branded apps to be a helpful resource to their ideal audience. Get any ideas on how you might use branded apps for your business?

SEO Basics for Online PR and Marketing

29

Search engine optimization (SEO) is the science and art of creating your online content so that it is easily recognized by programs such as Google and Yahoo. The goal is to enable the search engines to match your relevant content to users' search queries and return your content as high on the results page as possible, preferably on the first page of results.

SEO is an ever-moving target, because Google and the other search engines constantly refine their search criteria, in part to keep clever programmers from gaming the system. Though there is a never-ending effort by SEO professionals to add the latest tweaks that get search engine attention, there are also some core basics to help your Website and other online content make the most of search engine visibility.

The truth is, users rarely read beyond the first one or two pages of search results, and most never go beyond the first page. If your site isn't coming up near the top, you're missing out on prospects who know the generic terms for what they need, but don't yet know to look for your company or product by name.

SEO 101

Search engines such as Google and Bing use sophisticated programming algorithms to scour all the searchable content on the Internet in response to a user query and return the results in mere seconds. As incredible as that feat is, what is even more mind-boggling is that most of the time, the computers are able to return a dead-on match of sites for the often vague and generic keyword search typed in by the user.

When a user knows your company or product name, it's not too difficult for them to guess your Web address or to find you via the search engines. But millions of potential customers know that they need the sort of product or service you provide, but they don't know where to get it. These are the people who will type in phrases like "small business marketing," "driver education programs," "house cleaning services," and so on, looking for a solution. The companies that come up highest in the results, determined by the algorithm to be the most relevant to the search terms, are the ones the prospect will see first, and are likely the only ones he or she will see.

The job of SEO is to assure that your online content meets the relevancy requirements of search engines so that your information surfaces near the top of the results. Though the algorithms change frequently, at their core are two basics: relevancy and freshness.

Content is "relevant" when it closely matches the keywords typed by the user. Unfortunately, consumers rarely think in the same buzz words or terms that company owners use. Consumers tend to use more generic terms, and to avoid industry jargon. Many sites with the solution or product a user really wants may not show up in the search results because the company's Website copy doesn't match the user's keywords.

The trick here is to find out how the average customer/prospect would search for your type of product or service, and then to use those words frequently throughout your online content so that the search engines recognize your content as relevant. Fortunately, free tools such as Google Keyword Tool make it possible for you to find out how many searches are made on many popular terms. As I mentioned earlier in the book, if two terms are synonymous and one term gets a few thousand hits and another gets millions of hits, you want to use the more popular term. It's obviously a closer match to the way consumers think, and using the more popular term in your content will help your site land higher in the rankings.

Keywords are important, but so are tags. Tags are the captions you provide for photographs, diagrams, video and audio, content that isn't searchable for sites such as Google. Because search engines can't see pictures or video and can't hear audio, they either ignore them as blank spaces, or they must rely on the captions provided by the site owner.

Many site owners forget about captioning, missing an opportunity to repeat company and product names, book titles, event names, and the names of prominent individuals, even descriptive copy. These captions are powerful places to use keywords to help search engines recognize the relevancy of your site to the searcher's query.

Never pass up a chance to use a keyword in a meaningful way. Search engines also look at "anchor text"—the highlighted words that are hyperlinks to other pages. Make your anchor text do double duty as keywords. Instead of just putting "click here," use the name of the product or service, or the keyword generic description.

Search engines also look for freshness. They want to see sites that are frequently updated. Sites that have not been updated in weeks, months, or years drop in the algorithm because they aren't as fresh and therefore are judged to be not as relevant.

One way to keep your Website fresh is to have your blog or Twitter feed automatically update a place on your home page, so that you are simultaneously updating your Website every time your Tweet or post. Your Web designer can set this up using the RSS feed from the social media sites. The great part is that, once it's set up, the updates occur automatically, so you don't have to incur a Web designer's fee no matter how frequently you post.

You can also create freshness by being sure to regularly add upcoming events, product news, and other elements such as new video/audio, press releases, and awards/accomplishments. Make it part of your budget to add or update something monthly, and use the RSS automatic feed to bring your blog posts/tweets on a daily or weekly basis. With very little expense or effort, your site now goes from being static and irrelevant to being fresh and highly relevant. Remember to use your keywords to make your posts and tweets even more appealing to the search engines.

Tools to Make SEO Easy for the Busy Business Owner

Hiring an SEO firm can be expensive. Fortunately, there are a growing number of moderately priced and do-it-yourself tools to help you boost your SEO appeal.

Google Keyword Tool is a must-have part of your SEO toolkit. Use Google Keyword Tools whenever you're writing Web content, blog posts, social media updates and especially for online press releases. Choosing the more popular keywords and using them whenever relevant in your online writing can help your sites make a big jump upward in the search engine rankings. Always remember that you are writing for two audiences: human readers and search engines. Use the most powerful keywords as often as possible to please the machine, but keep in mind that human readers must also find the content compelling and natural.

WebSiteGrader.com is a site that provides a free snapshot of how your Webpage looks from and SEO perspective. It's a diagnostic tool that shows you what you're doing well, how you compare with other sites, and where you have room for improvement. You can take the snapshot back to your regular Web designer to address the weak points, or hire the folks at WebSiteGrader to do the job.

GoogleAnalytics is another free program that gives you a checkup on your Website's traffic sources, stickiness, bounce rate, and the keywords most often used by people who find your site.

Adzzoo.com offers a relatively inexpensive option for moving your Website higher in the search rankings. Through their proprietary process, the folks at Adzzoo create an extra, hidden Webpage that humans can't see but that is packed with relevant keywords and tags to be sure search engines recognize your page when a related search term is keyed in by a user.

MakeMeSocial.net is one of a growing number of one-stop-services focused on providing package SEO and social media content management for small businesses. For those who want to outsource their SEO and social media content management to someone else, MakeMeSocial is an option to consider.

Google Webmaster Central won't reveal every secret about Google's search engines, but the site was designed to help Website owners do a better job of optimizing their sites to rank higher on relevant searches. Bing and Yahoo have their own versions of this tricks-of-the-trade site, and it's worth checking them out every few months, because the search engines are famous for switching up their criteria frequently.

Remember to keep your budget, your top business goal, and your key target audience in mind as you interview SEO firms, as the process can be time-intensive and can get expensive quickly. Few firms beyond the very largest corporations can afford all the possible SEO bells and whistles. That being said, it is possible for smaller companies and solo professionals to afford a solid, basic level of SEO to improve their ranking results. As you budget, realize that SEO is not a once-and-done investment. Because the search engines are constantly changing their criteria, you will need to make regular updates to your SEO in order to maintain your good rankings.

Results Reminder

SEO is non-negotiable. If they can't find your online content, you won't get the sale.

The Rule of 30

What are the 30 words you use most to describe your company? Run them through Google Keyword Tool and see how they rank!

30

Exercises

1. After you've checked your most commonly used phrases against Google Keyword Tool, plan to make adjustments in your current and future online content to maximize your search results.

2. Have a discussion with your Web designer to be sure that all photos and not-searchable content (video, audio, and diagrams) are properly tagged with good, keyword-rich descriptions.

3. Determine what, if any, budget you have to engage an SEO firm. Even a modest, limited-time investment can yield big returns, so don't be afraid to start small and add as you are able to do so.

Where Do I Go From Here?

Online marketing and PR is constantly changing and evolving. As new promotional platforms emerge, and new services/programs are developed, the opportunities for online promotion will continue to expand.

Although the choices can sometimes seem overwhelming, keep your top business goal and your ideal target audience firmly in mind, and you will have a compass to find your best choices. Because online marketing and PR is still an emerging specialty, it will be up to you to be on the lookout for new tools, and to seek new ways to combine and leverage products.

Never lose sight of the fact that online marketing and PR offer tremendous opportunities to integrate your promotion with your social media outreach. Leveraging your online and offline marketing will also extend the benefit of your promotional campaigns and increase the effectiveness and duration of the bounce you receive. Always look for ways to have your marketing efforts in one area reinforce and build on your efforts in another area.

Remember that though online PR makes it easy and affordable for you to reach a global audience via the Internet, the real heart of publicity lies in person-to-person interaction. Word of mouth, whether in-person or via online comments and reviews, remains the most potent promotion.

Don't forget that there are people on the other side of the Internet connection, people who are reporters, reviewers, bloggers, social media friends, and ultimately, consumers. Although technology enables you to reach a wider audience than ever before, and ingenious programming makes it possible for search engines to find your content, the ultimate goal is to connect a person with a solution to the person who needs that solution.

~~~

For a free recap of the key points in this book and other extra content, visit *www.GailMartinMarketing.com* and click on the "Book Bonus Free Download" link.

Afterword

During a luncheon with the CEO of a regional, not-for-profit, community hospital system, I asked him, "How do you measure employee satisfaction? Do your employees feel like they are a part of the community? What are you doing to grow your employees and encourage their participation in the community outside of work?"

The questions were seemingly "off topic." I, along with three other local business owners, had been invited to break bread and talk about healthcare, how costs were impacting our businesses, how we viewed reform, how we were managing against changes to the system, and what things we were doing to provide good coverage to our employees in a period of significant change and debate.

We were there to hear about how the hospital and its affiliates could better serve the community and its patients through better systems such as electronic records management, improved access to hospital resources, or perhaps improved access to information about programs and services.

However, as I listened to the CEO define the hospital's mission, its reason for being a not-for-profit, why that made them different in approach and service, and why, in some respects, it made them more competitive in the marketplace compared to other for-profit hospitals he had managed, I began to wonder if everyone else in the hospital agreed. Did the market believe the message? Did the staff believe the message? Did the hospital marketing and PR department consider all of their audiences? While he very much believed the mission was clear and achievable, had everyone else bought in to the plan?

Businesses today face increased competition, fluctuations in marketing conditions, and an overwhelming need to be available to answer questions. Your brand, whether it belongs to a company, or it's your own, is more exposed and more debated than ever. Whether you compete for lunch traffic on a busy city block, need to fill beds at a hospital, or provide other businesses with goods and services to help them grow, customer expectations have changed.

In our inbound, always-on world, marketing and brand management rests in the hands of more than just the marketing department or business owner. Google, Bing, and other search tools, along with social platforms such as Facebook, Twitter, LinkedIn and YouTube, have given a voice and level of ownership and control to everyone in the organization and those it serves—whether you're in retail, finance, healthcare, or any industry—people and employees are talking. They are talking about you. And you have a need to be in control of that message.

How can you possibly get ahead of that curve? How could you, whether alone, or with a team, possibly manage all that chatter?

Back to our hospital CEO: What mattered for me in considering how the hospital could improve care in a changing landscape was whether or not the doctors, nurses, technicians, and other personnel *believed* in the hospital's mission. Did they themselves feel like a part of the community? Did they choose to work at a community hospital for the same reason the CEO had? Had they bought in to the hospital's goals and objectives for care and service?

The CEO's short answer was yes. They had internal surveys and high scores in employee satisfaction and positive press in the local media.

However, if I reviewed the online sentiment regarding the hospital, would the overall scoring be positive? If I drilled down to employee comments, would they match the internal survey results? If I examined comments from people that had received treatment, or were the caregivers of someone that had been treated at one of the hospital facilities, would their sentiment be positive as well?

Consider this: If we sat down together and I asked you to tell me how you felt about a product or service that I manufactured or delivered, would you tell me everything you felt about it? Would you be completely honest about the product's value as it related to the cost, quality, and level of service? Now, if you went online to a community forum where complete strangers were discussing the same product or service, might you say a few more things than what you shared directly with me? Importantly, how can do I gather those thoughts to improve, grow, and change?

The opportunity to build fresh, effective digital strategies requires marketers and business owners to use the tools available to them to listen, learn, adopt, and adapt in our "always on" world. And to start, you need top-down belief to ensure plans are properly executed and the integrity of the brand is maintained.

Whether you use online or social marketing and PR as a part of your overall strategy today, the tools and information are readily available to plan and implement a no-nonsense strategy. Marketing and public relations techniques haven't changed; they've just changed locations and swept up a few new ideas. You can compete and you can grow. This book will help make that happen.

—Josh Jordan
President
Makemesocial.net

Recommended Websites

www.1shoppingcart.com
www.adcenter.microsoft.com
(MSN Ad Center)
www.AdMob.com
www.advertisingcenteral.yahoo.com/SearchMarketing
www.AdWords.Google.com
www.AdzZoo.com
www.Alexa.com
www.Amazon.com
www.att.com
www.AudioAcrobat.com
www.AWeber.com
www.Bing.com
www.biznessapps.com
www.BlogTalkRadio.com
www.cculearning.com

www.cculearning.com
(Conference Call
University)
www.CityMax.com
www.CitySearch.com
www.CJ.com
(Commission Junction)
www.ConstantContact.com
www.Delicious.com
www.Digg.com
www.DivaToolbox.com
www.ebay.com
www.Elance.com
www.eSpeakers.com
www.EzineArticles.com
www.Facebook.com
www.Flickr.com

www.foursquare.com
www.FreeConference.com
www.FreeConferenceCalling.com
www.FreeConferencePro.com
www.Free-Press-Relase.com
www.Google.com/Adsense/
www.Google.com/Alerts
www.google.com/dfp/info/sb/
index.html
    (Double-click For
    Publishers (DFP) Small
    Business)
www.Google.com/Webmasters/
    (Google Webmaster
    Central)
www.GoogleKeywordTool.com
www.GoogleRankings.com
www.GoToMeeting.com/Webinar
    (GoToWebinar)
www.Groupon.com
www.Guru.com
www.hulu.com
www.imSMB.com
www.Jumptap.com
www.LATalkRadio.com
www.libsyn.com
www.LinkedIn.com
www.livingsocial.com
www.local.com
www.MakeMeSocial.net
www.OnAirPublicity.com
    (Wayne Kelly's)
www.Paypal.com

www.PicasaWeb.Google.com
www.PodcastAlley.com
www.PodcastPickle.com
www.PR.com
www.PRLeap.com
www.PRLog.org
www.PRNewswire.com
www.PRWeb.com
www.Quantcast.com
www.RadioGuestList.com
www.RingleaderDigital.com
www.Shutterfly.com
www.Skype.com
www.Squareup.com
www.Statbrain.com
www.Statsaholic.com
www.StumbleUpon.com
www.SurveyMonkey.com
www.tag.Microsoft.com
www.TalkFusion.com
www.TalkZone.com
www.Technorati.com
www.TinyURL.com
www.Twitter.com
www.VerticalResponse.com
www.Vimeo.com
www.Vistaprint.com
www.VoiceAmerica.com
www.WebSiteGrader.com
www.Xtranormal.com
www.Yahoo.com
www.Yelp.com
www.YouTube.com

Index

About the Author

Gail Z. Martin is an author, entrepreneur, and international speaker on marketing for small business and solo professionals. She owns DreamSpinner Communications, helping companies create better marketing results in just 30 days. She works with companies, coaches, consultants, authors/speakers, and nonprofits throughout North America. Martin holds an MBA in Marketing from The Pennsylvania State University, and has more than 25 years of marketing experience, including corporate and nonprofit senior executive roles. She founded DreamSpinner Communications in 2004.

Gail speaks to international audiences on social media, small business marketing, book promotion and defining success. Whether it's a keynote presentation, a workshop, seminar or breakout session, her high-energy, down-to-earth style energizes and provides a clear road to action.

Gail extends the strategies from her books through group and one-on-one coaching programs, teleseminars, custom consulting, e-books, and home study programs. Learn more at *www. GailMartinMarketing.com*.

In addition to *30 Days to Online PR and Marketing Success: The 30 Day Results Guide to Making the Most of Online Promotion to Grab Headlines and Get Clients*, Gail is also the author of *30 Days to Social Media Success: The 30 Day Results Guide to Making the Most of Twitter, Blogging, LinkedIn, and Facebook*, and *The Thrifty Author's Guide* series, which providers her unique approach to book marketing.

Gail is the host of the Shared Dreams Marketing Podcast where she interviews thought leaders, trendsetters and notable entrepreneurs and authors (*www.SharedDreamsPodcast.com*). She's on Facebook as Gail Martin, 30 Day Results Guide, and The Thrifty Author, and on Twitter @GailMartinPR. Gail is the co-host of the Big Dreams and Hard Work blog, sharing insights into social media and online marketing for small business (*www.BigDreamsAndHardWork.com*).

Gail is also the author of the bestselling fantasy adventure series *The Chronicles of the Necromancer* (*The Summoner, The Blood King, Dark Haven, Dark Lady's Chosen*) from Solaris Books and *The Fallen Kings Cycle* (*The Sworn, The Dread*) from Orbit Books. Find her fiction online at *www. ChroniclesOfTheNecromancer.com*.

Gail lives in Charlotte, NC with her family.

Contact Gail Z. Martin online at Gail@GailMartinMarketing.com